# What Happened
# in
# Education

# What Happened
# in
# Education

## An Introduction to
## Western Educational History

**T. D. BURRIDGE**

*Faculty of Education*
*McGill University*

Allyn and Bacon, Inc.                    Boston

Copyright © 1970 by Allyn and Bacon, Inc.,
470 Atlantic Avenue, Boston

Library of Congress Catalog Card Number: 70–116019

Printed in the United States of America

# Contents

# What Happened
# in
# Education

# Introduction

IF THE MAN IN THE STREET of a few decades ago had been asked to identify the main educational problem, he could have replied in a single word: provision. He would have meant that there wasn't enough of it freely available for his children. The popular cry, like that of Oliver Twist, was for more. People believed in education with a fervor akin to that which their fathers had devoted to God and Country, and almost as uncritically. The nature, purpose, organization, and methods of the subject were the preoccupations of a few. Otherwise, education was like an elephant—difficult to define, perhaps, but easily recognizable when you saw it. Even the majority of the teachers probably took the animal for granted.

Today, almost everyone is rather more aware of the educational elephant and not merely of its gigantic size. The moment at which an elephant is noticed tends to be a somewhat critical time. It is increasingly apparent to the

1

public, as well as to those professionally concerned with education, that the Oliver Twist response is not sufficient. Education involves moral considerations in the sense that what goes on in schools or other institutions stems from decisions about what ought to go on. These decisions may be more or less articulate, but the essential point is that they have to be made. Ultimately, therefore, the problems of education are philosophical, social, and political, and it seems clear that teachers, administrators, parents, and perhaps even the students are going to be more actively involved in the decision-making process than hitherto. For this reason the history of education has come to be an important part of teacher preparation, and it seems likely that the subject will command a more widespread interest in the future.

This interest in history is characteristic of modern Western man. Ever since the eighteenth century, when he became excited about the future, he has not been content with vague philosophical or metaphysical explanations of who he is or how things came into existence. Instead, he has turned to history and in so doing has considerably enlarged the concept of history itself. Not so long ago the main emphasis was upon what the great men had said or done and the political events in which they took part. Today the social, economic, and cultural background is given considerable attention, and, in particular, the education of an individual or a group is recognized as a significant factor influencing behavior and outlook.

But what is education? The answer varies from time to time and place to place. Its aims and methods are closely related to the values of the society that produces them, and if that society is in a state of profound change, the more disagreement there will be about education. Aristotle succinctly summarized this situation with the following remarks:

Mankind are by no means clear about the things to be taught, whether we look to virtue or the best life. Neither is it clear whether education is more concerned with intellectual or moral virtue. The existing practice is perplexing; no one knows on what principle we should proceed—should the useful in life, or should virtue, or should the higher knowledge, be the aim of our training; all three opinions have been entertained. Again, about the means there is no agreement. . . ."[1]

Such is the case today, and the widespread contemporary interest in the subject is a reflection of it. Since the Second World War the technological revolution has gathered momentum. In all Western countries this has already produced, and is likely to continue to produce, social and cultural changes that are fundamental, complex, and frequently bewildering. Institutions, beliefs, and values are now being challenged not so much by rival ideologies or political antagonisms as by the new material conditions in which we live. Nowhere is this more true than in the sphere of education.

The aim of the history of education is to illuminate and put into perspective the theories, practices, and problems of the present. There are certain risks involved. The past existed in its own right, and the past, after all, has passed. History doesn't repeat itself exactly. Nor can we any longer expect to discover a pattern of progress or even many clues as to the direction in which the present is moving. Unless one is a dogmatic Marxist or possesses some magical insight, he must accept the tentative nature of historical explanation and understanding. Indeed, there is nothing like history, unless it be travel, for narrowing the mind. Much depends on the way in which either is done.

Educational history raises the same problems of selection and emphasis as does any other branch of history. The subject involves the whole story of civilization, and many textbook writers have tried to include everything.

This essay has been devised as a brief introduction.

[1] Aristotle, *The Politics*, trans. B. Jowett (New York: Modern Library, Inc., 1943), bk. 8, chap. 2, p. 321.

Although it retains the usual chronological pattern, the intention is to suggest connections between what has happened in education and the issues that confront us today. The approach is therefore a subjective one, and comprehensive treatment of the subject is not its main function. Some of the stock heroes and villains will not be found here, nor will everyone agree with its interpretations. In a sense the views expressed are meant to be challenged, or at any rate pulled apart. Once the reader is doing this, the educative purpose of the book will have been achieved.

### SUGGESTED READINGS

#### Selected Anthologies of Primary Sources

Baskin, W. (ed.), *Classics in Education*. New York: Philosophical Library, Inc., 1966.

Cubberley, E. P., *Readings in the History of Education*. New York: Houghton Mifflin Company, 1920.

Gillett, M., *Readings in the History of Education*. Toronto: McGraw-Hill Company of Canada, Ltd., 1969.

Gross, R., *The Teacher and the Taught*. New York: Dell Publishing Co., Inc., 1963.

Johnston, B. (ed.), *Issues in Education: An Anthology of Controversy*. Boston: Houghton Mifflin Company, 1964.

Monroe, P. (ed.), *Source Book of the History of Education for the Greek and Roman Period*. New York: The Macmillan Company, 1929.

Nash, P., *Models of Man: Explorations in the Western Educational Tradition*. New York: John Wiley & Sons, Inc., 1968.

Ulich, R., *Three Thousand Years of Educational Wisdom*. Cambridge, Mass.: Harvard University Press, 1947.

#### Brief General Surveys

Beck, R., *A Social History of Education*. Englewood Cliffs, N.J.: Prentice-Hall, Inc., 1964.

Ulich, R., *Education in Western Culture*. New York: Harcourt, Brace & World, Inc., 1965.

### Additional General Surveys

Boyd, W., *The History of Western Education*. 7th ed. London: Adam and Charles Black, Ltd., 1964.

Brubacher, J. S., *A History of the Problems of Education*. New York: McGraw-Hill Book Company, Inc., 1947.

Butts, R. F., *A Cultural History of Western Education: Its Social and Intellectual Foundations*. New York: McGraw-Hill Book Company, Inc., 1955.

Jarman, T. L., *Landmarks in the History of Education*. London: John Murray, 1963.

Mulhern, J., *A History of Education*. New York: The Ronald Press Company, 1959.

Power, E. J., *Main Currents in the History of Education*. New York: McGraw-Hill Book Company, Inc., 1962.

### Other Books

Broudy, H. S., and Palmer, J. R., *Exemplars of Teaching Method*. Chicago: Rand McNally & Company, 1965.

Curtis, S. J., and Boultwood, M. E. A., *A Short History of Educational Ideas.* 2d ed. London: University Tutorial Press, Ltd., 1956.

Nash, P., Kazamias, A. M., and Perkinson, H. J. (eds.), *The Educated Man: Studies in the History of Educational Thought*. New York: John Wiley & Sons, Inc., 1965.

# 1

# Education
# and
# Historical
# Perspective

TECHNICALLY SPEAKING, history used to be the study of the past based on written evidence. Since records go back 7000 years, they cover an enormous quantity of human experience. Nowadays the historian is also interested in a great variety of nonwritten evidence. No one can consider education in the total perspective of history, as no one can know all of history. The historian must select some aspect or aspects of this experience that he believes to be of interest or significance. In our case, education is the aspect and the context is Western Civilization.

## CONCEPT OF WESTERN CIVILIZATION

It is not difficult to see or sense our historical continuity with the civilization that originated in the islands of the Greek peninsula and the desert margins of the Near East. This is expressed today in a legacy of ideas, values, beliefs, and institutions in many countries, and not least in the social activity called education. But this continuity must not be taken too literally. Unless there is a clear-cut philosophy of history, it is not easy to discern a simple, systematic pattern to events over 3000 years. Those writers who have tried to find one have had great difficulty in arranging the evidence to accord with their theories. Those who have not attempted to find a pattern have been obliged to limit themselves to more modest areas. Yet the concept of Western Civilization is valid for the educational historian because it is possible to associate many educational ideas and practices with it rather than with Eastern civilizations. And if, as Sir Kenneth Clark has pointed out, it is difficult to define civilization, it is fairly easy to recognize barbarism.[1]

### FORMAL AND INFORMAL EDUCATION

Again technically, education for the historian used to mean the formal, self-conscious, and more or less organized effort to bring up, nurture, rear, train, instruct, brainwash—if you like—the young. But as most learning is in fact acquired informally, the historian has come of late to broaden his horizons in this connection also.

However it is regarded, education is predominantly a social process. This applies whether it takes place only within the family (the most common social institution among all peoples of all times) or in a school. Its overall purpose is that of ensuring the survival of the individual and the customs, values, and ideas of the group.

#### Requisites for Formal Education

There are two requisites for formal education. One is that the group be sufficiently conscious of its cultural identity to want to preserve it; the other is that individual survival skills must have become complex enough to warrant a specialized learning situation. The more complex a society

---

[1] *The Listener* (London: British Broadcasting Corporation, April 24, 1969), p. 565.

is, the more there is to learn; the more there is to learn, the less likelihood there is of the individual being able to learn in an entirely casual, unorganized, and informal way.

Plenty of formal education goes on in primitive, preliterate societies. Maturity rites, for instance, are often much more elaborate and arduous than graduation exercises. But this type of formal learning is very similar in method to informal learning and lies mainly within the province of the anthropologist. The historian becomes deeply interested only when a written language has been developed.

### IMPLICATIONS OF WRITTEN LANGUAGE

Whenever writing is encountered in early civilizations, there are also schools and cities. This is no accident. People develop a written language only when their problems demand it, and urban societies are complex societies. This does not mean that every individual needs to understand the written language in order to survive. Far from it. The possession of literacy down through the ages has been in the hands of a tiny minority. Sometimes this minority has jealously guarded the secret; it gave them prestige and power. Until recent times there has been no necessity for *universal* literacy. The present attempt to achieve it began little over 100 years ago. It is a revolutionary undertaking in the history of mankind.

The social effect of the introduction of writing varies. Control and organization of people may be much more effective. Trade and commerce may expand. Knowledge is no longer in danger of being forgotten. A generation may now begin the struggle for survival armed with better accounts of past experiences and ideas. But all this may not in itself lead to change or progress in any fundamental sense. On the contrary, growth may be inhibited for long periods. Formal education may be limited almost entirely to the study of a few classical or sacred texts. The priceless product of civilization may be used exclusively by an elite to preserve the status quo, *their* status quo. Again, much may depend on the type of alphabet developed. It may be like that of the Chinese, of such difficulty as to require decades of application before any degree of mastery is acquired.

The achievement of universal literacy can produce similar ironies. If all the books and newspapers are controlled, far from freeing men's minds, the reverse may be true. Even where this is not the case, the question is sometimes raised, "What do most people actually read or write?" In an age when electronics is beginning to challenge the influence of the printed page, this question may have additional significance. Small wonder that some educational historians have begun to focus their attention on three stages in the development of communication: the alphabet, the printed book, and electronics.

## IMPLEMENTATION OF SOCIAL VALUES AND IDEAS

Important as communication devices are, they do not provide anything like a watertight formula for examining the history of education. They are but tools, and we are also interested in the use to which communication devices are put. This depends on the economic, social, and political structure of society, together with philosophical and religious ideas—or, in other words, what a society stands for, be it god, trade, liberty, war, universal brotherhood, or a continuous increase in the gross national product. The kind of work a school does, the social composition of its students, the amount of time they spend there, and other similar characteristics are related to what a particular society, state, or culture requires, permits, or encourages.

Any theory of education reflects a particular view of man and of human values, of society and of political relationships, of knowledge and how it can be acquired. Beyond this, however, the historian is concerned with seeing how these ideas are implemented in terms of curricula, institutions, and methods—both generally and in specific cultural contexts. Often there are fascinating and instructive discrepancies between theory and practice. Sometimes what appears to be a theoretical issue turns out to be a practical one, and vice versa. Individual philosophers and philosophies are not always consistent.

AGRICULTURAL VERSUS INDUSTRIAL
SOCIETY

Is it possible to find an initial concept or two that will enable us to establish some preliminary bearings? John Dewey, writing about the entire history of educational theory, declared that "it was marked by opposition between the idea that education is development from within and that it is formation from without."[2] For Dewey, the concept of education as "formation from without" was the old or traditional concept; the notion of education as "development from within" was of the modern era. This is a useful idea because it points to the two broad types of society in which formal education has been carried on. First there is the traditional variety, that is, the one in which agriculture is the main economic activity. ("Variety" is the operative word here. They differed greatly in respects other than economic.) Then there is the society with which we are most familiar, where industrial methods of production predominate. In turning from one to the other, the concept of survival undergoes a complete transformation, as indeed does the entire culture. In particular, the problems of education take on a new dimension. (At the present time it is possible to glimpse the beginnings of a post-industrial society, but for the sake of clarity a consideration of the latter's educational implications will be postponed until the last chapter.)

**Education in Two Societies Compared**

The traditional agriculturally based society consisted of "a mass of peasants with a greater or less urban superstruc-

---

[2] John Dewey, *Experience and Education* (Toronto: Collier-Macmillan, Canada, Ltd., 1963), p. 17.

ture."[3] It was led or dominated by a small group of people, and it was this group which received most of the formal education, especially that involving literacy. On the other hand, industrial society is essentially an "urban society with a peasant residue,"[4] and this residue is becoming very closely linked to the urban culture. Although modern society also has often been politically controlled by a fairly small group of people, membership in this group is generally not nearly so rigidly exclusive or self-perpetuating as in the agricultural community. The intellectual domination by those in political authority is mitigated by the greater complexity of modern society and the vast increase in the amount of knowledge. In fact, the only way such societies can function effectively is by widespread provision of formal educational facilities. It is this social characteristic which sets modern educational institutions apart from all others in the educational history of Western Civilization. This has not meant that educational or indeed other social ideas and practices have not been carried over from the first kind of society; educational obsolescence has occurred very often in history. It does mean, though, that a major part of the history and philosophy of education so far has concerned itself with the education of a tiny minority.

### Children in the Traditional Society

Most children in the traditional society were reared for the purpose of work, and manual work at that. They constituted the vital human reserves that were required in the never-ending struggle for existence. These children were not devoid of all education; very often they actively participated in a rich folk culture. They were born into a more integrated society than ours, although exaggeration has to be avoided; it is easy to sentimentalize the folk culture and pastoral community. The point here is that these people received

[3] Raymond Aron, *The Industrial Society* (New York: Frederick A. Praeger, 1967), p. 18.
[4] Ibid., p. 18.

little or no *intellectual* education. They could not read or write. Even the children of the elite group were not indulged sentimentally. They were regarded primarily as political and economic links in the social chain of inheritance. Their marriages were social and economic contracts, arranged for them at an early age. Excessive feeling for children in the traditional society was limited by the fact that very many of them died in infancy or early in life. The concept of childhood as having a dignity and character of its own belongs to the modern world.[5]

### Education of the Elite

The education of the minority group in the traditional society was governed by the fact that, more often than not, these people belonged to an aristocracy, secular or religious, within a rigid class structure. Most upper classes, once they had established themselves, had at least two things in common: a certain amount of leisure time and the necessity of maintaining their social leadership both in times of war and in times of peace. The education of young males (the females were usually excluded) bore a definite relationship to these factors. In our time, particularly as a result of automation, opportunities for leisure appear to be growing spectacularly for all classes of people. Moreover, the problem of providing a suitable education for leadership, or for choosing leaders, remains. We may therefore have something to learn, in a surprisingly direct way, from the educational experience of societies and peoples who at first glance appear very different.

Partly because of education's historical link with elite groups, it has usually represented a conservative social force. This explains to some extent why educational institutions, practices, and ideas have shown such a remarkable

[5] Philippe Ariès, *Centuries of Childhood: A Social History of Family Life,* trans. Robert Baldick (New York: Random House, Inc., Vintage Books, 1962), pp. 33–49.

resistance to change. Yet the same is true even in our own time and may always be so in some degree. After all, parents can hardly be expected to acquiesce passively to proposals to educate their offspring in some revolutionary manner. This was particularly the case in the traditional society: you would anticipate your grandchildren having much the same type of life that your grandparents had had. Few indeed are those parents willing to heed Bernard Shaw's advice that if you have to hold yourself up to your children as anything, do it as a warning, not as an example.

### Educational Consensus

Elitist-type societies had fewer difficulties than we do in defining the specific aims of education. Confining education to their own relatively homogeneous group, the aristocracy could proceed to instruct their children in those areas considered relevant to their particular way of life, regardless of other sectors of society. Today, given the feeling or conviction that everyone ought to be educated, any kind of consensus on the purpose, nature, and organization of such education is extremely difficult to achieve. Such consensus is almost impossible in *any* type of society in a state of change, and one of the chief characteristics of modern society is the speed of change. In the traditional society, education was usually organized on a voluntary, private basis; contemporary society has had to introduce a strong element of compulsion, with the state playing the dominant role. Variety, flexibility, and experiment are often hamstrung in the very type of society where these qualities are most needed.

### The Knowledge Explosion

There is another basic difference between the two types of societies. Prior to modern times there was only a limited amount of "knowledge" to be acquired. Even if the means of acquiring that knowledge were restricted to a few people, it was conceivable that one person might comprehend all there was to know. From about the seventeenth century on, this has not been the case. In the emerging post-industrial society, despite the communications revolution, the extent and depth of the "knowledge explosion" have been such that schools, teachers, and students are faced with what is considered to be a new educational situation. Strictly speaking, this is correct, but one of the fascinating aspects of educational history is that *somewhat* similar crises have confronted society before.

## SUGGESTED READINGS

Ariès, Philippe, *Centuries of Childhood: A Social History of Family Life*. Translated by Robert Baldick. New York: Random House, Inc., Vintage Books, 1962.

Carr, E. H., *What Is History?* Middlesex, England: Penguin Books, Ltd., 1964.

Compton, Neil, "The Paradox of Marshall McLuhan." *New American Review*, January 1968, pp. 77–94.

Dewey, John, *Experience and Education*. Toronto: Collier-Macmillan Canada, Ltd., 1963.

McLuhan, Marshall, *The Gutenberg Galaxy*. Toronto: University of Toronto Press, 1962.

——, *Understanding Media: The Extensions of Man*. New York: McGraw-Hill Book Company, 1964.

Myers, E. D., *Education in the Perspective of History*. New York: Harper and Brothers, 1960.

# 2

# Education
# in the
# Ancient
# World

An EDUCATIONAL CRISIS that was just as fundamental as anything we have to face occurred in Greece (more specifically, Athens) in the fifth and fourth centuries B.C. It has affected the theory and practice of education in Western Civilization from that time forward—an instance of that historical continuity mentioned previously. Yet we must beware of making a false analogy.

### ANCIENT GREECE

The conditions of life in those Greek city-states of over two millennia ago were not only different from our own but also unique, in some respects, in the ancient world itself. No doubt these differences can be exaggerated. Two of them, for example, that strike us rather forcibly are their use of slaves and the small size of their communities. "How slow the pace of life must have been," we are tempted to think.

"With the slaves doing all the work, little wonder that those Athenians seem to have spent most of their time in long philosophical discussions, sports, political disputes, theatres, and wars. What else was there to do?" But continuity there has been. What else do *we* do? And it has been estimated that Athens at one point had a population of approximately 300,000 people. Many of the contributions of the Greeks are widely acknowledged, but Greek education and ourselves? One may well ask whether a connection exists.

### Aristocratic Values

The development of Greek society, both before and after the time of their (and our) great poet Homer, follows a pattern not unlike that of other primitive agricultural and essentially patriarchal communities. At first the important values were those of personal courage, honor, reputation, and achievement. These were the values of those persons who, by virtue of superior physical strength, will, cunning, effort, and probably some luck, managed to arrive at the top rank of society. What mattered most was doing something better than anyone else, and at this stage of social development, the deed was usually performed on the battlefield.

The ideal that motivated the education of their (male) offspring was thus individual excellence and prowess. This was more important even than loyalty to society, and the Greeks had a word for it, *areté*. Later on, when society settled down, when the city-states established themselves, the aristocratic ideal of areté merged with that of loyalty and obedience to a particular polis, or, as we might say, good citizenship. At this point the aristocrats had recognized that the good life could only be obtained via the political unit of the city-state. It also signifies their recognition of each other as a class within a society.

### Aristocratic Education

These two stages in the evolution of an aristocracy relate to its preoccupation with leadership and leisure noted earlier. At first, education placed its emphasis on the production of future leaders and military leaders at that. Gymnastics was at the core of such a curriculum. Later, the leisure aspect became increasingly important, but this was not leisure in the modern sense of free time. This was an aristocracy that still had a social function to serve, especially in time of peace. This function was not merely one of decoration but of active political and cultural leadership. Here the other two staples of the traditional Greek curriculum began to play a part in the proper upbringing of the young: grammatical studies, necessary for passing on the mythological and religious heritage in which the aristocratic ideals were now enshrined (necessary also for practical purposes), and music, an essential requirement for gracious social living, involving the skills of singing, playing, and dancing, as well as the dramatic arts.

This subject-centered education was both cultural and vocational. It developed spontaneously and un-self-consciously over a long period of time. Its subsequently celebrated qualities of harmony and balance, the healthy mind in the healthy body, were the entirely natural products of genuine social needs and were closely related to actual life. There was no system to it; this type of education involved no set curriculum and no final examinations. It was a private, personal, and voluntary business, the individual tutor being the formal instrument of the process. There must have been a great variety to this education in quantity, quality, and duration. Again, it was not for the few but for the very few.

### Schools

By about the sixth century B.C., private schools had come into existence. This may indicate that some of the less affluent members of the aristocracy found it cheaper to send their boys to a school than to engage a tutor. It also testifies to the degree of social awareness among the Athenian upper classes, because schools provide a broader instrument for the socializing of the young than do private tutors. It is significant that our word "school" comes, via the Latin, from a Greek word meaning "leisure," that is, freedom from political and economic activities. Only those who enjoyed such freedom could attend a school, and one of the reasons why the Greek aristocrats appear to have regarded the teachers as inferior beings was that they had to work for a living. It can also be noted here that these early schools played but a small part in education. The slave—the pedagogus—who accompanied the boy to and from school and who protected him and looked after his welfare generally had an important role in a boy's upbringing. In comparison, the teacher was merely a skilled technician. One of the most striking features of contemporary education is the increased scope in the role of the teacher, which at times beggars description, ranging from nursemaid to father-confessor.

Not much is known of the earliest of Greek schools beyond the fact that regulations were made for the protection of the boys. These regulations were also concerned with the protection of the adults, but they did not apparently pertain to the buildings, since one early reference reports that a roof collapsed on the boys while they were being taught. However, buildings presumably would not have been much of a problem in that sunny climate. The special schools for gymnastics, the palestra for elementary exercises and the gymnasium for more advanced work, were open-air structures anyway, and the gymnasium was publicly sponsored. The grammatical, literary, and music studies all took place in the music school, which, with the probable addition of some elementary arithmetic, takes on the character of what we identify as a school.

Here the master taught and the pupils learned—that is to say, copied, memorized, imitated. The maintenance of discipline would not appear to have been difficult. Apart from corporal punishment, the boys were continually under the watchful eyes of the pedagogus. Acquisition of skills in the various subject areas provided a foundation for character building, moral training, and awareness of civic responsibilities, for the subjects studied had a direct relationship to the kind of social life in which the boys were about to participate. As someone has said, the Greek definition of an idiot would have been an absolutely self-centered, private man. The elementary instruction of a boy's early years was rounded off in late adolescence by an equally relevant training in military and civic affairs, at the conclusion of which the young man was required to swear a loyalty oath to the polis, so help him Zeus.

### Religion

The question of Greek religion and its relationship to education merits a word of explanation. It consisted, for the most part, of some fascinating stories about all-too-human gods (male and female) and a temple or two. The theological aspect was not highly developed, and therefore the religion did not require a body of teacher-priests. Nevertheless, its influence was a strong one. This was because the religious ceremonies were, in effect, civic ceremonies. The supernatural powers of the gods were invoked on behalf of the polis. In becoming a good citizen, the Greek youth was also demonstrating a proper respect to religious authority. No conflict arose between state and church in regard to education; the latter's predominantly secular character accurately reflected the position of religion in Athenian life.

In short, then, and also in idealized retrospect, the famous harmony of Athenian education resides in the balance between its physical, aesthetic, and intellectual content, between its individualistic and social aim, between its as-you-like-it type of organization coupled with tacit state encouragement, and between its strict attitude toward the boys while at school combined with their daily return to a more friendly home atmosphere.

### SPARTA

Compared with this picture, Sparta provides an extreme contrast, an educational case study of lasting interest. This is because education there came to be subordinated exclusively to government policy. Having had a much tougher struggle over man and nature to establish themselves, the Spartans bought their eventual victory by the creation of an authoritarian militaristic régime. This régime sought to perpetuate itself by means of a totalitarian political and educational system. Despite the unpleasantness of the latter, people have continually found redeeming features in it, down to our own times.

The main reason is to be found in the essentially conservative character of Spartan society, product as it was of fear and insecurity, a position with which some people can always be found to sympathize. The Spartans did, however, carry this to an extreme, or so it would appear. Any and all change was suspect and resisted. They were opposed to both democracy and tyranny. Their culture provided the classic example of austerity and physical severity. Apart from patriotic stories, songs, and dances, there was no aesthetic cultivation. The Spartans clung to a backward economy despite a relatively fertile soil and iron ore deposits. Their main social virtues were the military ones of obedience and bravery, and living at Sparta was like living in an armed camp.

### Spartan Education

In this situation the Spartan education system—it is possible to speak of a system here—was controlled by the state. Its single aim was the production of brave and obedient soldiers. Its methods were practical and activist: part of the final examinations involved the "personalized" killing of a local slave. That they were successful in achieving their aim is best illustrated by the immortal story of the Battle of Thermopylae. Sparta continued to produce soldiers of that quality for over 200 years.

The historical importance of Spartan education is its demonstration of the *power* of an education system. This is the reason for its emotional appeal. In its simplicity, order, discipline, and stability it offers hope for people who live in insecure and confused periods. No matter that it was bloody, brutal, miserable, and intellectually bankrupt; these aspects will be overlooked.

One other lesson may also be drawn: there may be certain dangers involved in the desire to have perfect clarity in the definition of educational purposes. The process of education involves human relationships, and if these are narrowly circumscribed, much creativity may be lost.

## ATHENS

This can be understood when the Athenian educational crisis of the fifth and fourth centuries B.C. is considered. Historical factors there had given the Athenians an almost bewildering amount of experience and variety in human relationships. Politically, for instance, Athens since the formative period had been the home of aristocracy, monarchy, tyranny, enlightened and unenlightened despotism, as well as partial democracy. The city had become an urban and cosmopolitan center and the Athenian world had been transformed. Colonies had been established around the Mediterranean in Asia Minor, Italy, and Sicily as Athens became a maritime and commercial power. Athenian society drastically changed. Increased opportunities, for instance, had broadened the ranks of the aristocracy, giving wealth and leisure to a wider class of citizens. Two new social groups, the urban middle and working classes, vied for power with the aristocrats. Political troubles at home and abroad were as familiar to the Athenians as they are to ourselves.

These changes had a tremendous impact on the former establishment values. The old athletic ideal was ridiculed. The civic religion was held in contempt. "Man," individual man, "is the measure of all things," was one cry. Moral relativism, coupled with an unabashed popular materialism—a chase of the almighty drachma—developed. In reaction to this, for a period of some fifty years from about 479 B.C.,

Athens witnessed an extraordinary outburst of intellectual and artistic creativity.

### Educational Crisis

The Golden Age of Athens radically affected education. The former training was now patently obsolete. Or was it? Conservatives naturally said no and complained bitterly about the frivolity of the new subjects, a complaint that has been echoed since in other places. What had happened was that the former elementary curriculum (as it may be loosely described) had become more intellectual, more literary, more widespread, and, in conservative opinion, less concerned with morality and character formation. The physical aspect of the old education had lost much of its force also. Indeed, athletics itself had become more professional, and a not-unfamiliar tendency to spectator sports had developed. But the major educational changes affected the areas we regard as secondary and post-secondary.

Under the old dispensation there had been little in the way of secondary schooling at all. There was a gap between the palestra and the music school and the military-citizenship training beginning at eighteen years. True, a boy could have learned, and probably did learn, a great deal by simply walking around the streets and public places with his father or tutor during the intervening period. And interestingly enough, this practice has been recommended by a contemporary American critic of education: "Dispense with the school building for a few classes, provide teachers and use the city itself as the school—its streets, cafeterias, stores, movies, museums, parks, and factories."[1] Yet the brighter and more ambitious of the youth were no longer satisfied by this informal type of secondary education. They, or their parents, demanded a more didactic intellectual apprenticeship.

---

[1] Paul Goodman, *Compulsory Mis-Education and the Community of Scholars* (New York: Random House, Inc., Vintage Books, © 1962), p. 32.

### The Sophists

These demands were met at first by an itinerant body of teachers, usually foreigners (non-Athenians), who came to be called Sophists. These instructors or lecturers first appeared in Athens around 450 B.C. To the diehards, the Sophists were the Dale Carnegies of the ancient world, purporting to teach courses in how to win friends and influence people. What the Sophists themselves claimed to offer, for a fee, was a specialized training in leadership and social success. Apart from other objections, the aristocrats must have been offended that no particular hereditary prerequisites were deemed necessary. So long as you could pay the money, you took "the course of your choice." Ironically, only sons of aristocrats or wealthy men could have afforded the time and fees. Yet the impact of the Sophists upon education has far transcended the shock they caused to some members of the Athenian nobility in the fifth century B.C. When the Sophists declared that rhetoric or public speaking was the answer to the question "What knowledge is of most worth?" the traditionalists of the time believed that this completely ignored the moral aspect of education. A similar response from traditionalists greeted the educational views of the first humanists and scientists, as well as our own innovators who argue that the most important "knowledge" is neither rhetoric nor philosophy nor theology, nor classical languages nor science, but "knowing how to learn." Perhaps there's a moral in this. At any rate, the impact of the Sophists on the subsequent history of education has been a fundamental one. They stimulated the first theoretical discussion of the subject in Western Civilization.

### Isocrates

Many of the Sophists must have rejected the specific charge that rhetoric was a subject in which it didn't matter what you said, as long as you were convincing. At least one of them, Isocrates (393–338 B.C.), counterattacked with lasting effect.

> Those who desire to follow the true precepts of this discipline may, if they will, be helped more speedily towards honesty of character than towards facility in oratory. And let no one suppose that I claim that just living can be taught; for, in a word, I hold that there does not exist an art of the kind which can implant sobriety and justice in depraved natures. Nevertheless I do think that the study of political discourse can help more than any other thing to stimulate and form such qualities of character.[2]

It is important to note that this comes from a tract called *Against the Sophists*. Isocrates was well aware that some of his fellow teachers were either charlatans or did not understand that rhetoric was not merely a bag of technical tricks but a creative process. In his defense of rhetoric as the key subject, Isocrates raised deeper questions—of a type very similar to those asked by his near namesake, Socrates. What ought to be the nature, purpose, and content of education? Isocrates managed to achieve something of a practical link between all of these; he saw rhetoric in ethical terms. At the same time he was essentially a teacher; he recognized the importance of innate ability and declared that while subjects such as geometry and astronomy were of little value in themselves for most people, they did provide a useful preliminary intellectual discipline. In sum, he strongly believed that education was concerned with concrete problems and had to be rooted in the practical. The great abstract philosophers, Socrates, Plato, and Aristotle, largely disagreed. Surprisingly, however, the professional educator's position was not adversely affected by this conflict. In the opinion of the famous French scholar Henri Marrou, it was Isocrates and not Plato who "educated fourth century Greece and subse-

---

[2] Isocrates, *Against the Sophists*, trans. G. Norlin. Quoted in *Models of Man*, by P. Nash (New York: John Wiley & Sons, Inc., 1968), p. 63.

quently the Hellenistic and Roman worlds."[3] It must be noted, though, that rhetoric eventually came to mean classical literature, and Isocrates' original aim of producing men of *action* was sometimes overlooked. Still more significant to those with a democratic turn of mind is the fact that the Sophists, by implying that leadership could to some extent be learned, held out the promise that many men could benefit; through education everyone could create his own culture. The celebrated Greek concept of *paideia*, the complete man, the cultured man, begins with the Sophists, even if, as Marrou[4] has indicated, it reached its fullest expression in Hellenistic times. The Sophists did not share the philosophical view that education should have no utilitarian aim. On the contrary, they implied that education could be both vocational and cultural simultaneously, a view closer to the older Greek outlook. The attempt by the philosophers to drive a wedge between cultural and vocational aims in education was the real innovation. A contemporary parallel in reverse is evident in a certain tendency to conceive education in narrow vocational terms, as the production of efficient technicians.

## THE GREEK PHILOSOPHERS

Socrates, Plato, and Aristotle were also teachers, of course, and Socrates was one of the greatest teachers who has ever lived. But these men were intellectuals and scholars foremost. They were seekers after wisdom and lovers of knowledge for the sheer joy of it. They taught because they had to, whereas Isocrates is reputed to have made a fortune. This is not to be construed as prima facie evidence against the latter's sincerity. It merely points up the differences between him and the great philosophers: he was temperamentally the kind of man who attempts to come to terms

[3] H. Marrou, *A History of Education in Antiquity*, trans. G. Lamb (New York: Sheed and Ward, 1956), p. 79.

[4] Ibid., pp. 97–100.

with the world as he finds it, which involves compromise and expediency. They, in more senses than one, were idealists and geniuses as well. They sought definitive answers to the problems of education and to life itself. There is both splendor and arrogance to be found in this.

For the Greek philosophers, ethics automatically involved political and social considerations. It has to be reiterated that the polis, or community, had come to have a religious significance besides the political one. The good life, it was believed, could only be found within the city-state; the question of individual happiness had to be resolved within this context. But much had happened to the city-state. The old civic gods, mythological heroes who had been the backbone of the former aristocratic citizen values, were no longer accepted. The new order of things had to be devised by the reasoning power of man alone.

### Socrates

This in itself did not bother Socrates (469–399 B.C.), who approached such matters in an open-minded, even pragmatic, way. What did worry him was his conviction that the old values had been replaced by a vulgar, intellectually shallow creed of selfish opportunism and materialism, and the old education by instruction in the art of glib speech-making, a mere tool to be used in a dog-eat-dog struggle for self-advancement. He set himself in the marketplaces and squares of Athens to expose the new clichés as false and dangerous to the well-being of society, a position that carried its own trait of egotism. But Socrates' attitude was that he himself knew nothing and simply sought to know the truth. This, he implied, was education, the individual quest for knowledge and wisdom. Being a man of prodigious energy and single-mindedness, he devoted himself to the task. In relying on reason instead of falling back on some mystery cult or other, he gained immortality.

His method was not calculated to bring him immediate popularity. It involved, first, the reduction of a student to a state in which he confessed his own ignorance. This was achieved by means of a series of penetrating questions, usually concerning some abstract ethical proposition. By the end of the series the student was led to contradict his earlier responses. Thereafter, Socrates would develop his own theory of the truth, getting the student to assent to each stage of the argument. The underlying implication of this method was that true knowledge is obtained solely through the dialectical process of abstract reasoning. This, in turn, stemmed from Socrates' idea of what true knowledge *was*. In his view, knowledge was a system of everlasting and perfect *ideas* that existed independently of the material world. The ultimate idea was that of the "good." These ideas could not be apprehended by the senses; they were perceived only by abstract reasoning. Aristotle basically shared Socrates' (and Plato's) theory of knowledge, but Aristotle did pay some regard to material, scientific evidence. This difference was to occupy much of the philosophical controversy in the Middle Ages and persisted in educational discussions at least until Francis Bacon's enunciation of the scientific method in the seventeenth century.

What Socrates did not seem to realize was that people simply do not like being made to feel ignorant and stupid, and the practical effect of his teaching was often the reverse of what he intended. It only seemed to add to the confusion of the day and in the end led to his death on the charge of corrupting the youth. From our lofty historical perch, we cannot say that this reaction was abnormal. In spite of his enormous personal charm, Socrates was in some respects a naive and therefore irritating man. As a teacher he undoubtedly overlooked the effect of what he said on the students (and their parents). To demand total honesty and consistency from ordinary people is to demand the impossible. Nor did he find the answers that he was seeking, perhaps because he asked the wrong kinds of questions.

As far as education is concerned, his argument, briefly, was that philosophy ought to be the key subject. Individual man had to be trained in the use of his reason so as to distinguish right from wrong, truth from falsehood, etc. The old elementary instruction was not enough; poetic examples of noble conduct, exercises and music, exhortations to emulate the actions of the heroes for the benefit of the polis: all these would not ensure that men would act wisely. But if the study of philosophy was rigorously pursued, then the essentially ethical aim of education, the production of good and just men, might be achieved. This followed from Socrates' ideas about the immortality of the soul and his theory of knowledge.

### Plato

At this point it becomes increasingly difficult to differentiate the ideas of Socrates from those of his student, Plato. Most of what we know about Socrates comes from the writings of Plato because Socrates never wrote down anything. This is not of material consequence to us except insofar as Plato's social and historical position caused him to take Socrates' initial thoughts considerably further.

Like Socrates, Plato (429–348 B.C.) was an intellectual, but unlike him, a born aristocrat with a strong emotional attachment to elitist views. This meant that Plato, disillusioned equally with the democratic and the aristocratic experiments of his time, was rather more prone to view education in a political and social context. It is clear that Plato shared Socrates' theory of knowledge, which distinguished between the "real" spiritual world and the "shadowy" material one. Similarly, Plato agreed that as man's immortal soul already "knew" everything, education was basically a process of rediscovering this knowledge, the bringing of an individual to as full an awareness of ultimate spiritual reality as possible. Once this had happened, the individual could be relied upon to pursue the good in all things. Plato saw this very much as a political problem: how could society be organized so that this could occur? The solution, Plato believed, lay with the state. Only the state was capable of carrying out the education of men thoroughly enough to produce a good society.

Given the idea that perfect knowledge brought with it, or meant, moral perfection and that such a sublime state was attainable, then Plato's answer is logical. Unfortunately for us, the modern scientific view of knowledge is that it is morally neutral. This explains why many a contemporary scientist declares that whatever use is made of his discoveries is for society to decide. Thus the fundamental philosophical problem of politics—how to ensure that only good and reasonable men be entrusted with power—remains essentially as Plato described it.

Being an aristocrat, Plato was not as afraid of the state as we might be. He looked back nostalgically to the good old days when society was more orderly and balanced. In those days the aristocracy had dominated the state. However exaggerated and idealized this attitude was, we can easily recognize the sentiments involved.

### The Republic

Plato's famous book *The Republic* is an attempt to provide a rationale and a sketch of such an ideal society. Rejecting democratic values, the book supports the idea of aristocracy, but an ideal, intelligent, and educated aristocracy, as being the only way of achieving the perfect society. His book is one of the greatest literary masterpieces that Western Civilization has produced, and the study of philosophy virtually begins with it. Although it would be presumptuous to attempt a discussion of *The Republic* here, a few of its educational ideas and implications can be indicated.

The most obvious of these is the connection between education and politics: the fact that most of the subsequent educational thinkers in Western Civilization have been political theorists as well (for example, Aristotle, Rousseau, Locke, and Dewey) is eloquent confirmation of the concept's durability. It is not the logical demonstrability of a particular view of the state or society, however, that is educationally important, but the attitude toward education that it contains and the actions such a view stimulates and motivates. Plato's own mystical view of the state, for instance, has had a marked influence on aristocratic and totalitarian societies. From this point of view, cultural greatness does not depend on, say, the amount of wealth, freedom, or equality possessed by individuals. Rather, it depends on the subservience of individual wealth, freedom, and equality to some higher ideal. Plato held that the state must seek to inculcate its young with proper ideas and beliefs and, furthermore, protect them from alien influences. The modern liberal-democratic tradition tends to look with suspicion, if not antagonism, at any direct attempt on the part of the state to promote morality, on the grounds that it tends to destroy the moral autonomy of individuals. Nonetheless, the problem is still there. All modern states underwriting education systems insist on having some say in the character formation of their future citizens. The question is, To what extent and by what means?

Because Plato was distrustful of the moral and intellectual capacities of most human beings, he recommended an extreme solution. The masses were to be brought up on propaganda and "noble lies," whereas the ruling elite were to receive a long and thorough training in logic and philosophy. This means that his (or Socrates') theory of knowledge was modified somewhat to take into account the varying capabilities of individuals. It is not necessary to accept his theory that human beings come in basically three intellectual sizes (regular, king-size, super) to see that a comprehensive system of state-provided education raises a problem of selection. The most suitable education for all cannot be the same education for all. How then is the state to choose or provide for choice, particularly if certain facilities are lacking, as they always seem to be? This, again, is a question that remains with us. Plato's answer was to make a basic elementary education available to all and then to eliminate gradually those deemed unsuitable for higher education by a series of tests. Unfortunately, he was not very specific about the mechanics of the latter, and it is extremely doubtful whether the former would have been as democratic in practice as it may sound.

Plato's totalitarian views also underline a problem of much contemporary interest. Not only would he have the schools subjected to the strictest censorship, but the rest of society also. The values transmitted by the schools were to be reinforced by what might be called the other communications media in society. What contemporary teacher is not aware of the impact of television, radio, and newspapers? Plato has made it impossible to overlook the fact that education raises cultural as well as political problems of fundamental importance, that it is silly to consider education without reference to this wider framework. Yet people like Isocrates at the time were able to show that the totalitarian answer was not the only one. Both men agreed that education was necessary for individual happiness and social well-being. Both agreed that it should seek to develop character. Isocrates, while recognizing that this would not necessarily help someone of a depraved nature, was content to leave it at that. Plato could not. He sought perfection, at least for a few people.

In so doing, he illuminated many other aspects of education, including some that were either forgotten or ignored and have but recently emerged. Instances are his recognition that females are equally capable of benefiting from education, the attention he gave to emotional and aesthetic development as well as intellectual, his concern about each item in the curriculum from an overall point of view, the importance he attached to preschool education, and his awareness that education had to proceed in stages corresponding to the growth of the child. Furthermore, because he saw education as the chief task of government, he recognized that teachers ought to receive a special training and be carefully chosen. They were among the most important servants of the body politic. There are many teachers today who will vouchsafe that this is still not generally recognized or, if given lip service, not acted upon.

Liberal Education

Undoubtedly one of the most lasting effects that Plato has had upon education comes from his idea of "liberal education." Originally education arose from the relatively un-self-conscious aristocratic tradition in which formal intellectual training was the prerogative of the ruling and leisured class. As we have seen, this had both a cultural and a vocational aim. What Plato did was to define education in terms of a purely theoretical training in logic and philosophy based on grammatical, literary, and mathematical studies that were to have no particular practical or technical application—except insofar as this training was to lead *eventually* to philosopher-kings or rulers. Contrast this with the Sophists' stress on immediate relevance. The conflict is as alive in the contemporary university as it was 2500 years ago. Should education concentrate on how to live the good life or on how to earn a good living? Or can it do both? Plato's opinion was quite clear: education was a training in virtue, *not* "that other sort of training, which aims at the acquisition of wealth or bodily strength, or mere cleverness apart from intelligence and justice."[5] This educational ideal he deemed the only one appropriate for a "freeman," someone who was free in an economic sense as well as a legal one. Such a general training would fit an individual for the duties of decision-making that might fall to him and also for the life of contemplation and philosophical speculation that would occupy him in the quest for wisdom. Symbolic of this ideal was Plato's transfer of his classes from Socrates' public squares and marketplaces to the more secluded Groves Academius; hence derived our pejorative use of the word "academic" to mean unrealistic or unworldly, and thus also the notion that any vocational, technological, or even scientific education is somehow unworthy of a gentleman and is

[5] Plato, *The Laws*, trans. B. Jowett. In *The Dialogues of Plato*, 2 vols. (New York: Random House, Inc., 1937), 2:424–25.

anyway inferior to a classical education—a notion that, although now intellectually dead, still refuses to lie down. At the same time, it must be emphasized that Plato did not imagine an advanced technology such as ours. His objection to technical training was that it did not represent a true culture of the whole man.

### Aristotle

It is noteworthy that Aristotle (384–322 B.C.), Plato's most celebrated student, in spite of the fact that he lived later and differed in intellectual interests from his master, also defined ethics in terms of the state. Man, he believed, was primarily a political animal; he was "born for citizenship." Aristotle also did not hesitate to accord to the state powers that we find extreme, including that of regulating the best ages for marriage, which he reckoned to be eighteen for a woman and thirty-seven for a man! More important, it was the duty of the state to legislate morality and happiness as well as the conditions necessary for these to exist. But he recognized that there might be different forms of states and systems of education, as long as the two were closely related. He knew that difficulties would arise if there was no basic agreement within a society. A main task of an education system in his opinion, therefore, was that of mitigating and eliminating such disagreements. The social function of education was to transform an amorphous group of people into a community wherein an individual could find a full and happy life as well as security.

Aristotle, in fact, gave more emphasis and attention to the needs of the majority of individuals than did Plato. The aim of education ought to assist the individual achievement of happiness. Instead of trying to fit each person into a particular social slot, education should take account of psychological as well as intellectual differences. Too much concentration on any one aspect of education, even intellectual training, would not be the wisest policy: "Some liberal arts [are] quite proper for a freeman to acquire," he said, "but only in a certain degree"; and again, "No doubt . . . children should be taught those useful things which are really necessary," such as reading and writing, "but not all things."[6] The pursuit of individual excellence in any field had to be tempered with the need for socially desirable behavior. Aristotle was closer to the original aristocratic ideal than was the revolutionary Plato. In addition, he was a man of many more parts, more diverse interests, and more aware of the complexities of individuals and societies. He was not such a perfectionist; his literary style does not dazzle, but he does exhibit more of that quality of inestimable value in any discussion about education, common sense.

Even so, this has not prevented his views from attracting the attention of many hostile critics from the seventeenth century to the present. What has particularly irritated these critics has been the unequivocal support that Aristotle gave to Plato's distinction between liberal and illiberal education. It is true that Aristotle was mainly concerned with the formation of the well-rounded gentleman-citizen, a nonprofessional but an informed amateur capable of sound judgment and good taste in all matters. After our recent surfeit of educational specialization, there may be grounds for a reconsideration of his aim. Furthermore, just as it will be later argued that modern progressivist theories do not axiomatically exclude much of what Aristotle had to say regarding the *content* of liberal education, so it may be noted that Aristotle was by no means the only advocate of the latter to suggest some very activist *methods*. He claimed, for instance, that both theory and experience were necessary components of the learning process.

Although Aristotle has to be understood in his historical context, many of his other views are still pertinent. It wasn't enough that an education system be supported by legislation alone; to be really effective it needed the cooperation of a

[6] Aristotle, *The Politics*, trans. B. Jowett (New York: Modern Library, Inc., 1943), bk. 8, chap. 2, p. 321.

culture that valued objects of beauty and of intellect. One wonders what he might have said about commercial television. Both Aristotle and Plato valued education for leisure and leisure for its own sake. Nowhere is this more evident than in their stress on the importance of music in the curriculum. The development of the emotions was seen as a key factor in education, much too important, one might say, to be left to Tin Pan Alley and local radio stations. Of course, even in those days there was a debate about what constituted good music, but Plato and Aristotle considered the school's job was to influence taste in this matter. Their opinion that the schools must not merely reflect popular values but instead be the chief social agency for uplifting and changing them has been echoed in the twentieth century by John Dewey, among others.

The emphasis here has been upon the opinions of the Greek philosophers about education. Yet it should not be overlooked that their major influence on Western education has not come from these directly. It was the whole body of their philosophical and scientific works that provided the staple element in the curriculum for so long. These works were given an excellent launching into educational history by the higher schools of research and philosophical learning originally founded by the philosophers themselves, the academy and the lyceum—words that are still synonymous with education in many countries.

### THE GREEK EDUCATIONAL LEGACY

The educational legacy bequeathed by the ancient Greeks to Western Civilization was indeed a formidable one. Here, in embryo, we can recognize the pattern of our own formal institutions. Here the evolution of specialized teachers and subjects began. Above all, it was in fifth- and fourth-century Athens that our theory of education originated. All subsequent educational discussion had its beginning then, and much of it has not progressed very much further. Finally, it can be said that the Greeks provide us with an example of the relationship between education and the wider social and cultural environment from which we may still learn. Of this they were confident at the time, in Isocrates' words:

> Our city has left the rest of the world so far behind in philosophy and eloquence, that those educated by Athens have become the teachers of the rest of mankind; and so well has she done her part, that the name of Greece seems no longer to stand for a race but to stand for intelligence itself, and they who share in our culture are called Greeks even before those who are merely of our own blood.[7]

This legacy was given first to the world of the eastern Mediterranean area by the conquerors of the Greek city-states. By a famous historical irony, the loss of political independence helped rather than hindered the Greek cultural influence. The educational language of this vast area became Greek, and Greek institutions were widely copied. Centers of study and research such as Rhodes and Alexandria became almost as celebrated as Athens itself.

### The Seven Liberal Arts

The elimination of the polis meant that it was the Sophist educational tradition and not that of the idealist philosophers which was passed on in practice. The latter were to make more of an impact on the Christian world with its conception of the city-state of God. In the Hellenistic world, meantime, removed from the creative impulse of the old polis, or perhaps overwhelmed by it, learning everywhere became pedantic, more specialized, and comparatively sterile. Whereas the city-state had created its own literary and intellectual culture, the Hellenistic civilization was content to imitate, collect, classify, analyze, and only

---

[7] Isocrates, *Panegyricus.* Quoted by Matthew Arnold in "Equality." In *The Portable Matthew Arnold,* ed. Lionel Trilling (New York: The Viking Press, Inc., 1949), p. 585.

rarely enlarge or develop. A fixed group of subjects emerged as being most appropriate for the training of the young. It was divided into two sections: the language element, consisting of grammar, rhetoric, and dialectic (logic); and the scientific element of arithmetic, geometry, astronomy, and music. This curriculum was passed to Rome, becoming known as the seven liberal arts, although its liberating quality became less and less apparent. No doubt many a Roman boy came to regard them as the next thing to slavery.

### The Idea of Culture

Yet if the curriculum during the Hellenistic period tended to become stereotyped, the period, as Marrou has indicated, deserves to be remembered for its formulation of the ideal of the cultured man, which, all in all, may be considered as the most important single contribution to educational thought that has come down to us from ancient Greece. This culture was, in the final analysis, a personal possession, that which accrued to a man as a result of his individual attempt to explore the nature of truth. In a very real sense it took the place of the old religion; its distinctive characteristic was not merely the acquisition of knowledge for its own sake but the possession of a certain moral elevation. It was a man's culture that set him free, and this freedom could never be lost. Formal schooling played a relatively small role in what was considered a lifelong process. It was something of an educational disaster that this noble ideal became so closely identified with an ossified type of schooling.

### ROMAN EDUCATION

This was especially the case with the Romans. Early Roman education, like that of the Greeks, was homemade and usually took place there. It also put the emphasis on personal, political, and military conduct patterned after revered and idealized ancestors. But the Romans lacked poets of the stature of Homer and Hesiod. Greek intellectual culture was so superior that after the conquest of the Hellenic world the Roman youth was made to swallow the Greek curriculum wholesale, in Greek. It is little wonder that Roman schools, when they appeared, were by all accounts so much more brutal than Greek schools. Even when the Republic produced its own literary and intellectual culture, Greek influence predominated. Cicero's *De Oratore*, which appeared in 55 B.C., reflected the Roman equivalent of paideia, *humanitas*, and expressed educational opinions similar to those of Isocrates. *Humanitas* meant a combination of sound moral character with abstract, mainly literary, learning. It referred to a style of living, thinking, feeling, and acting; there was no dogma to it, no specifically religious consolation. It involved Stoicism—self-control, courage, rationality—as well as aesthetic sensitivity. This ideal was reiterated during the Empire period by the other important Roman writer on education, Quintilian (c. A.D. 35–c. 95). His book *Institutes of Oratory* is even closer to Isocrates than was Cicero's, perhaps because, like the Greek, Quintilian was a practicing teacher. Through the works of the Romans, the Greek rhetorical school of education was to influence directly the Europe of the Renaissance period when men were again to seek secular educational models.

There is little originality in Roman education. Mainly, the Romans standardized and spread the Greek model throughout Western Europe. They did attempt to provide public support for schools. Several emperors appointed professors, usually of rhetoric or law. Quintilian was among these. In addition, efforts were made to get the municipalities to support schools and teachers. But the Latin grammar school usually required fees from students, thus limiting enrollment to sons of wealthy families, and although many grammar schools were established, they did not constitute what we would regard as a comprehensive state system of education. Two peculiarly Roman contributions to education were the creation of special colleges of law and the sharpening of the social distinctions among the various levels of teachers. Both of these educational results of the Roman genius for organization have remained with us, the first beneficial, the other a more invidious relic.

## SUGGESTED READINGS

### Selected Primary Sources

Aristotle, *The Politics.*

Cicero, *De Oratore.*

Isocrates, *Against the Sophists.*

Plato, *The Republic.*

Quintilian, *Institutes of Oratory.*

(See also Selected Anthologies of Primary Sources listed at end of Introduction.)

### Other Books

Beck, F. A. G., *Greek Education, 450–350 B.C.* London: Methuen & Co., Ltd., 1964.

Carcopino, Jérôme, *Daily Life in Ancient Rome.* Middlesex, England: Penguin Books, Ltd., 1956.

Castle, E. B., *Ancient Education and Today.* Middlesex, England: Penguin Books, Ltd., 1961.

Crossman, R. H. S., *Plato Today.* New York: Oxford University Press, 1939.

Gwynn, A., *Roman Education from Cicero to Quintilian.* Oxford University Press, 1926. Reprint. New York: Teachers College Press, Columbia University, 1966.

Jaeger, W. W., *Paideia: The Ideals of Greek Culture.* 3 vols. New York: Oxford University Press, 1939–44.

Kitto, H. D. F., *The Greeks.* Middlesex, England: Penguin Books, Ltd., 1951.

Marrou, H., *A History of Education in Antiquity.* Translated by G. Lamb. New York: Sheed and Ward, 1956.

Nettleship, R. L., *The Theory of Education in "The Republic" of Plato*. Chicago: University of Chicago Press, 1906.

Popper, Karl, *The Open Society and Its Enemies*. Rev. ed. Princeton, N.J.: Princeton University Press, 1950.

Price, Kingsley, *Education and Philosophical Thought*. Boston: Allyn and Bacon, Inc., 1962.

Smail, W. M., *Quintilian on Education*. Oxford University Press, 1938. Reprint. New York: Teachers College Press, Columbia University, 1966.

Winn, C., and Jacks, M., *Aristotle*. London: Methuen & Co., Ltd., 1967.

Woody, T., *Life and Education in Early Societies*. New York: The Macmillan Company, 1949.

# 3

# The
# Christian
# Medieval
# Legacy

FOR OVER A THOUSAND YEARS after the collapse of the Roman Empire, the dominating influence in the theory and practice of formal education was the Christian religion. Indeed, for most of this time, education was not only controlled by the church but was almost solely for clerics. One of the results in the modern era has been the conflict between church and state over both the control and the organization of education and also its purpose and content. To best appreciate this it is necessary to glance back into medieval times to see how Christianity developed its interest in education, and what it came to mean in practice.

## THE COLLAPSE OF THE ROMAN EMPIRE

The political and economic breakdown of the Empire meant the breakdown of the conditions under which the old education had existed and which it had purported to serve.

This refers in particular to the decline of urban life in the Western half of the Empire. The cities there were in any case more artificial communities than those in the East. In origin military camps, they were consuming rather than producing cities in both a cultural and an economic sense.[1] Most of the population, wealth, and intellectual culture of the Empire was to be found in the Eastern towns. These managed to exist as political entities far longer than those in the West, and it was in them that Greco-Roman culture was best preserved. The most famous, Constantinople, did not fall to the Turkish Moslems until 1453. It was therefore the Western Empire that collapsed most dramatically. The area reverted basically to a primitive agricultural economy and tribal form of society. The only important institution to survive in any widespread form was the Christian religion, and even this was seriously affected by the almost total political insecurity and disruption of communications. Recently historians have discovered that much human activity did in fact go on from, say, A.D. 500–800, although this period has not been called the Dark Ages unjustly: little went on intellectually.

### THE ADVENT OF CHRISTIANITY

Christianity was not, in any case, much interested in education at first. Its appeal was an emotional one directed at the illiterate poor of both East and West. Learning was associated with the importance of reason in human affairs, an educational tradition derived, as we have seen, from Greek culture. The early Christians rejected pagan culture and the learning that went with it. Even the first educated pagans became converts precisely because they had lost their belief in reason. "I believe," said one of them, "because it is absurd," that is, unreasonable. Saint Paul himself considered those who still sought for worldly knowledge and wisdom as being foolish. One Christian leader, Tertullian, was even more explicit.

---

[1] C. Dawson, *The Making of Europe* (New York: Meridian Books, Inc., 1956), p. 106; H. Trevor-Roper, *The Rise of Christian Europe* (London: Thames and Hudson, 1965), pp. 46–47.

I call thee not as when, fashioned in schools, trained in
libraries, fed up in Attic academies, thou belchest forth
thy wisdom. I address thee simple and rude and unlet-
tered and untaught, such as they have thee who have thee
only, that very thing, pure and entire, of the road, the
street, the workshop.[2]

But not all the fathers of the church found such a direct
approach to grace possible. When Saint Jerome retired to
the desert to meditate on the evils of the world and the glory
of God, he took his pagan library, among other comforts,
with him. Occasionally giving way to the temptation of
reading poetry, his reaction was to write torrents on the
sinfulness of reading.

The very worldly success of Christianity heightened the
problem. From the basis of the Holy Scriptures, a sacred
literature developed. From the early peasant converts,
Christianity spread to the upper and educated classes in the
Empire. From being the simple faith of small groups of
fanatic believers who welcomed martyrdom, it became the
official religion of the state; and it created its own dogmas,
rituals, and institutions. How were the demands of the faith
to be equated with the practically necessary uses of reason,
and what kind of education would be required to service the
solution?

#### Augustine

The Christian who first attempted a comprehensive
answer to these questions was Saint Augustine (354–430), in
the fourth and fifth centuries A.D. He happened to be a well
and widely educated pagan of 34 who had espoused several
philosophies in his youth. When he turned Christian, his
view of education was that an old-fashioned grounding in
the liberal arts was as essential for a Christian as for a
pagan. The difference should lie in the purpose to which
such training was directed. For a Christian this purpose

[2] Tertullian, De Testimonio Animae, I, trans. Roberts and Donaldson.
Quoted in The Making of Europe, by Dawson, p. 61.

could only be a deeper understanding of the scriptural message. Preliminary studies should be regarded as mere tools that would facilitate this aim. But the logic of this position obliged him to add Greek and Hebrew, besides Latin, to his proposed curriculum. Augustine then had to warn "studious and able young men" who "feared God" and who "were seeking for happiness in life, not to venture heedlessly upon the pursuit of the branches of learning that [were] in vogue beyond the pale of the Church of Christ."[3] At heart he remained a mystic. An education could help explain the scriptures, but only faith could make them entirely meaningful. Faith did not depend on understanding; understanding depended on faith.

The Christian view of education followed from its conception of man as pre-eminently a spiritual and moral being, created for the divine purpose of testifying to the glory of God. As the way to redemption and salvation lay through faith, education's task was to strengthen this faith. It was the duty of the church to decide what kind of knowledge was necessary. Here the Christian parted company with the pagan. Even Plato was not willing to circumscribe knowledge in this way, at least for his elite; the more knowledge a man possessed, the more virtuous he became. For the Christian, man needed God's help, as interpreted by the church. Ironically, just as Augustine was proposing his solution, the necessary conditions for any learning were beginning to disappear. The various Christian schools of higher learning rapidly became isolated, resulting sometimes in varying interpretations of the gospels, some of which were subsequently deemed heretical.

### The Monks

During the centuries of the so-called Dark Ages that followed, the one organized institution that did manage to

---

[3] Augustine, *On Christian Doctrine*, trans. J. F. Shaw. Quoted in *Models of Man*, by P. Nash (New York: John Wiley & Sons, Inc., 1968), p. 100.

survive over a wide area was the monastery, the communal home of those hermits and mystics who wanted to be alone. The monks swore vows of poverty, chastity, and obedience and devoted themselves to prayer. The monastery was essentially an institution dedicated to the spiritual, not the intellectual, life. Still, the monks could not pray twenty-four hours a day, and Saint Benedict's rule, the one most widely copied in the West, was devised to keep them from temptation and the possibility of sin every moment when they were not actually at their devotions. One requirement was the reading of sacred works, from which practice has arisen a somewhat exaggerated idea that it was the monks who kept the torch of learning and education alight through the Dark Ages. In fact, what they mainly preserved was literacy and books; they excelled at copying. It is true that they also wrote chronicles and lives of the Saints from time to time, but this work cannot support comparison with that of the ancients. As some scholars have pointed out, the credulity and ignorance of the monks were immense, if for no other reason than that they were so physically isolated.

The great exception occurred in the most isolated part of Europe—the "bogs of Ireland." It was there that knowledge of the Latin and even of the Greek classics was best preserved. In the eighth and ninth centuries, monks from the Irish and English monasteries returned to the mainland of Europe to convert the barbarians and educate the ignorant. Famous examples are Saint Boniface, who converted the Germans, and Alcuin, who taught Charlemagne.

### Monastic Schools

At first, however, the educational work of the monks was largely confined to themselves. Society tended to be divided along Platonic lines: there were those people who, like the monks, prayed; there were those who fought; and there were those who worked. Oversimplified as this is, it does suggest the highly compartmentalized social structure of the early medieval period. Such education as there was reflected the predominant vocational function of each group and was extremely specialized. As some of the monastic orders began to succeed in an almost modern sense, to become prosperous and to found branches, a need for basic skills grew. Novices had to be instructed; records had to be kept. In addition, the monasteries often undertook charitable work. Inevitably they began to operate schools, even though the curriculum was limited to practical necessities such as reading, writing, counting, and singing.

In time two developments occurred. First, the liberal arts pattern reasserted itself, except that rhetoric in this context meant letter-writing and record-keeping. Second, some of the monastery schools accepted pupils who did not intend to become monks, perhaps in order to placate a local ruler. Even so, this remained a paramountly religious education, for the world was unimportant and might, indeed, come to a sudden stop at any moment. The training was anti-intellectual, anti-aesthetic for the most part, and undoubtedly anti-physical in its orientation. Its mechanical and authoritarian nature probably meant that methods of instruction were rather crude, if not brutal. The Christian concept of original sin and distrust of the flesh helped to sustain the ancient custom of corporal punishment in schools. The fact that the language of instruction, Latin, was foreign to most pupils did not help matters. The purpose of monastic education was to serve God, not man.

### Other Vocational Training

A similarly narrow vocational emphasis can be seen in the training of a knight. This changed from a type of military apprenticeship to a relatively sophisticated personal and social training, as necessitated by the chivalric ideal. It also was an exclusive process, as were the training programs of the merchant guilds. Such social unity as existed was provided by Christianity. This unity did not attain its highest point until the thirteenth century, when the secular power of the church was at its peak. Only then did the socializing influence of the church, expressed through its control of education, become really effective.

## FLOWERING OF THE MIDDLE AGES

The unifying power of religion exercised through education does become much clearer from roughly the year 1000. The failure of Charlemagne or his successors in the ninth century to bring religion and education under a political umbrella is less striking than the fact that the attempt was made. From this point on, the chaotic conditions of the Dark Ages gave way to a recognizably Christian civilization. By the end of the eleventh century, the barbarian invasions had been absorbed into its framework, the Moslem threat had been beaten back, and political and economic feudalism had begun to pay dividends of some surplus production and greater political cohesion, notably in France and in England. A revival of urban life began, the inevitable result of which was a growth in intellectual life. This coincided with an increase in knowledge in the West, mainly via contacts with the Arabs and other peoples: the Dark Ages of Europe were the Golden Ages of Islam. The Crusades were partly responsible for these cultural contacts, and at the same time they are indicative of ferment in Western society. The rediscovery of Aristotle, in particular, was to make an enormous impact upon the Christian outlook. The aristocracy developed an epic poetry. Yet, since the only organized and widespread literate groups were the clerics of one kind and another, it is not surprising that they were at the center of the new interest in learning and education.

The question that Augustine had had to face soon arose. What sort of learning was appropriate to a Christian? The church had now become a secular power with vested interests in both the material and spiritual worlds. How could these interests be reconciled? In the ensuing debate it is possible to catch an echo of the difference that had divided Plato and Aristotle. This medieval controversy, of limited interest now perhaps, nevertheless produced the most important institutional aspect of our educational legacy from the period—the university.

### The Cathedral School

Not unexpectedly, neither the monasteries nor the monastic schools had much to do with this. The university developed from the activities of the "secular" clergy—those who lived in the world—and not from the regular clergy, who lived by a rule in the cloister, which is an interesting sidelight on the ivory tower idea. (The latter concept is most applicable to the university in the eighteenth century, when it reached its lowest intellectual level.) In the absence of schools, the bishop had had to instruct his own clergy in his cathedral. Some preliminary education might also have been provided by a lesser priest to a limited number of boys who could sing, in what was called a *schola cantorum*. It, too, was connected with a cathedral, though perhaps taking place in a local church in a cathedral city. But by the twelfth and thirteenth centuries, various councils of the church were calling for every cathedral to provide organized training for future priests in a grammar school and to make more specific provision for the teaching of theology. When the bishop found that his educational duties were taking up too much of his time, he delegated them to a church official called a chancellor. The latter's responsibility was to appoint and supervise the specialist teachers who eventually emerged from the early beginnings of the cathedral school, as it was called. In fact, until about the ninth century all that was involved was the teaching of elementary subjects similar to those in the early monastic schools, but from then on, the liberal arts curriculum was gradually introduced. Because of the intellectual ferment in the church, the process did not end there. In some cathedral schools certain outstanding teachers attracted students from far and wide and ranged beyond the usual school curriculum. The fact was that Christianity was becoming so complicated that it needed a long period of study under specialist teachers to be fully understood, and during the period from the eleventh to the thirteenth century such study seemed to raise as many questions as it resolved. Much the same situation, but without as much conflict perhaps, existed in regard to disciplines such as medicine and law, as a result of the increasing knowledge available in the West and of the more complex social problems. All this meant an increasing demand for the services of those specialists who could devote themselves entirely to advanced subjects. The subsequent social pressure on the chancellor caused him to permit certain teachers to hire rooms away from the cathedral school in order to teach more effectively. In time these teachers formed themselves into an association similar to a guild and known by the generic name of *universitas*. The great advantage of such a collectivity was that it afforded protection to individual members. The historical significance of these associations of teachers is that they indicate a lessening of the hitherto direct control held by the church over educational organization.

### The Medieval University

In fact, it was not long before the universitas sought and obtained a measure of autonomy from the parental body of the church. In order to become a teacher it was not sufficient to have only a general teaching license from the chancellor. One had to be approved by the universitas, a practice that has continued to the present. Such autonomy was not obtained without a struggle. The chancellors did not meekly acquiesce in the transformation of their role to the formal and ceremonious one of awarding the licenses or degrees, although it is necessary to exclude here those instances in which the chancellor was elected as a constitutional head of the masters (teachers), in which case he retained certain administrative powers. Such elections took place in a general assembly of the masters known as convocation, which came to be the chief assembly of the university. With the growth in size of modern universities, convocation also has come to have a largely ceremonial role, its original function being superseded by a senate or other body controlled by the more senior teachers and sometimes including nonacademics as well.[4] There is little doubt that this latter arrangement is much less democratic than the old convocation, although the question as to what extent and in what ways the university can be democratic is a controversial matter. Nowadays the students demand a right of representation on the decision-making bodies of the university, as was certainly not the case in medieval Oxford or Paris, where the democracy was limited to the masters.

The autonomy of the university, like that of other medieval guilds, was given legal recognition by the granting of a charter of incorporation from king, municipality, or pope. As the teachers were still clerics, the charter from the pope was the most coveted. Sometimes such a charter was obtained despite the active opposition of the local authority, even if this happened to be the bishop. Among the self-governing powers granted by a charter might be exemption of teachers and students from property taxes and military service, determination by the university of its own curriculum, power of trial and punishment by the university over misdemeaning students, and the right of the university to strike against or even move away from a particular locality. This provision was often used in the celebrated town-versus-gown disputes. Some argue that such disputes are inevitable from time to time.[5] That the medieval universities eventually obtained such a large measure of legal independence was due to the intellectual reconciliation achieved in Western Christendom by the thirteenth century.

### Aquinas

The complex details of the theological crisis, and its resolution by Saint Thomas Aquinas (1225–74), may be

---

[4] In the United States the nonacademics have often been businessmen. On the continent of Europe the universities have been closely linked to the state. Only in Britain have the universities retained something of their old autonomy, and this has been threatened in recent years by financial dependence on the state.

[5] Paul Goodman, *Compulsory Mis-Education and the Community of Scholars* (New York: Random House, Inc., Vintage Books, 1962), p. 172.

studied elsewhere. The crux of the matter was that Aquinas succeeded, in the eyes of medieval Europe and of the Roman Catholic Church thereafter, in differentiating between the secular search for knowledge and wisdom that we call philosophy, and the study of revealed truth or sacred philosophy known to us as theology. The systematic and logical way in which Aquinas argued from abstract principles down to the minutest details deserves to be at least sampled by the reader in *Summa contra Gentiles* or *Summa Theologiae*. It was not without cause that he became known as the "angelic doctor." The chief purpose of the university after this was clear: it was to teach, explain, and illustrate the Aquinas thesis, which became the basis of the church's doctrine. Other functions of the university took a subservient place. The faculty of theology became the superior faculty. And so the "autonomy" of the medieval university came about because its aim was directly related to the purpose of European civilization as a whole. Today the function and position of the university in society are ambiguous to the degree in which the aims of society are ambiguous or pluralistic.

### Student Power

While the medieval reconciliation was working itself out, the issue of student power was a particularly lively one. Nowhere did the students have it so good as at the University of Bologna. There they selected and dismissed the masters, fined them for unpunctuality or sloth, imposed a salary cut if a master attracted fewer than five students, and charged heavy caution money to guarantee attendance at lectures and completion of contract. In addition, the students, by actually leaving the town en masse on several occasions, forced the authorities to abandon any attempt to control dress or behavior at festivals. But Bologna was an exception, though not uniquely so. There the university was created by the students themselves, and these students were no ordinary students. They were fairly well-to-do lawyers who came together to further their knowledge in the light of changing conditions. We would call them postgraduate students. They came to Bologna because a strong legal tradition had been preserved there since the establishment of a law school in Roman times.

In the more usual medieval pattern it was the masters who decided the rules and regulations affecting students. Each student paid his fee to his particular teacher and was regarded as an apprentice. No provisions were made for his lodgings or general welfare at first, and conditions for study were extremely poor. There were no permanent university buildings or property, and books were few and prohibitively expensive. In the absence of organized sports or amusements, student life was often rowdy, violent, and dangerous. When students fought among themselves or against the townsmen, it was sometimes to kill. In 1355 a riot broke out in Oxford, for example, that could hold its own in terms of violence with any contemporary fracas. Some sixty students were killed, a sizeable proportion of the total number in those days. Swords and daggers were taken to demonstrations—and all this despite the fact that many were studying or at least highly interested in theology![6]

### The University Curriculum

All students began with the faculty of arts course. The trivium, or language aspect of the curriculum, was left to the cathedral or grammar school, and by the end of the thirteenth century the quadrivium (the sciences) had come to be largely replaced by logic and philosophy, mostly Aristotle. The full arts course took seven years, and the failure or dropout rate must have been high. According to one teacher, the recipe for successful study was "a humble mind, zeal for

[6] In his *Rise of Universities* (Ithaca, N.Y.: Cornell University Press, 1957, p. 34), C. H. Haskins indicates that there were but few students of theology at the medieval university, and that a prescribed course in the subject came in only with the Counter Reformation. While this is so, it can be assumed that most medieval students were interested in theological questions and in this sense can be said to have been studying theology.

inquiry, a quiet life, silent investigation, poverty and a foreign land."[7]

Students began university as young as thirteen years. Halfway through the course a student became known as a baccalaureus—someone not yet a master but who could claim some academic standing, roughly the equivalent of a journeyman in a craft guild. The bachelor, as he came to be called, could be permitted to do some teaching. Upon completing the entire course, as part of the final ceremony, the student was required to give a specimen lesson, the "masterpiece." Then he (for all students were males) would be crowned with a master's cap and thus become entitled to teach the faculty of arts course at any university. The academic world was rather more international then than now, linked as it was by the church and the Latin language. One variation on the above outline was found at Cambridge University, where it was possible, apparently, to become a master of grammar after perhaps five years, which entitled one to teach at a grammar (high) school only. The graduation ceremony in this case included, besides the specimen lesson, a specimen caning, with the university providing both cane and boy. The aspirant teacher had to pay for both facilities.

It was only after completing the arts course that more specialized training could be undertaken. There were three possibilities—theology, law, or medicine—and of these, theology was the most difficult and lengthy. It took at least another seven years, whereas the other two disciplines could be mastered in four or five. The doctorate in theology required a further two years. These three disciplines acquired, over the centuries, a prestige that in Catholic countries has never been entirely lost. Their pre-eminence reflected the hierarchical view of subject matter derived from both the Greek thinkers and Aquinas. The notion that abstract subjects are intrinsically more valuable than practi-

[7] Hugh of St. Victor [twelfth century], *On Studying and Teaching*. Quoted in *The Portable Medieval Reader*, ed. J. B. Ross and M. M. McLaughlin (New York: The Viking Press, Inc., 1949), p. 583.

cal ones has had a very long life in the history of Western education.

## Teaching Methods

Similarly, teaching methods at the university level have changed remarkably little down through the ages. There were basically three methods at the medieval university: the lecture, the repetition, and the disputation. The key method was the lecture because of the acute shortage of books. There were two fairly distinct kinds of lectures in those days, the quick and the slow. The former was a free discussion of the text, the latter a dictation of it. The repetition, a discussion led by a senior student of the two sorts of lectures, bears a striking resemblance to the contemporary conference group taken by a postgraduate student. But it may well be regretted that the disputation, a kind of debate between two or more students presided over by a master, no longer seems to be with us. All these methods were well suited to the conditions prevailing at the time. Apart from the general scarcity of books in a book-starved age, the authoritarian nature of the curriculum has to be borne in mind. Scholasticism entailed the deduction of truth from accepted authorities, and the main job of the university was to pass on the church's position and the reason for it. Rote learning can hardly have been taken much further. Some time passed before people realized that the most effective method of ascertaining the number of teeth in a horse's mouth would be to look in it instead of in Aristotle. Some argue that comparable situations can be found in many of today's schools.

## Development of Medieval Educational Institutions

One of the side-effects of the emergence of about eighty universities in Western Europe by 1500 was a boost in the creation of secondary grammar schools. Indeed, by the fourteenth and fifteenth centuries the foundation of divers public and municipal schools is evidence that the church was falling behind social demand in its educational provision. But here again, the usual conception of traditional secondary schools as being solely a preparation for university is to be treated with caution. Some of the new municipal schools were founded to provide an adequate education in themselves. William Shakespeare is perhaps the most outstanding graduate of such a school, even though he improved considerably on the "little Latin and less Greek" he obtained there.

The medieval university was a guild or community of scholars, a trade union of intellectual craftsmen that functioned in much the same way as the associations of merchants or skilled workmen. It bore, or came to bear, a fairly specific relation to the relatively homogeneous society that produced it. Much of what was studied and learned so diligently now appears bizarre and irrelevant. But that it was relevant to its own time is apparent, if only to judge by the number of occasions when the university was requested to provide guidelines in difficult social, legal, and doctrinal matters. Even today we retain many of the ceremonious and symbolic aspects of the medieval prototype in our institutions of higher learning. Yet, amidst our current debates over the organization and function of our own universities, it would be misleading to lean too heavily on the original model as an ideal. It has to be remembered that medieval society possessed, at least in theory, an ideological unity that we cannot claim, at least outside of the totalitarian countries. This unity, however, was purchased at the price of a certain intellectual sterility that was to blight education for a long time. On the other hand, medieval education can be said to have had at least one special merit, given the circumstances, which renders it worthy of our attention. It did seem to be applicable to all sorts and conditions of men. Some historians declare that more educational opportunity existed in the Middle Ages than until quite recent times. While no one can be certain about this, there does exist one late fourteenth-century source which makes the following assertion:

> Now may every cobbler set his son to school, and every beggar's brat learn from the book, and become either a writer and dwell with a lord, or a false friar to serve the Devil. So that the beggar's brat becomes a bishop, to sit esteemed among the peers of the land, and lord's sons bow down to the good-for-nothings, knights bend to them and crouch full low, and this bishop's father a shoemaker, soiled with grease and his teeth as tattered as a saw with champing leather.[8]

### SUGGESTED READINGS

#### Selected Primary Sources

Aquinas, *Summa Theologiae.*

——, *Summa contra Gentiles.*

——, *The Teacher.* Translated by R. W. Mulligan, J. V. McGlynn, and R. W. Schmidt. Chicago: Regnery, 1954.

Augustine, *Concerning the Teacher* and *On the Immortality of the Soul.* Translated by George G. Leckie. New York: Appleton-Century-Crofts, Inc., 1938.

——, *Confessions.*

——, *The City of God.*

Ross, J. M., and McLaughlin, M. M. (eds.), *The Portable Medieval Reader.* New York: The Viking Press, Inc., 1949.

(See also Selected Anthologies of Primary Sources listed at end of Introduction.)

#### Other Books

Copleston, F. C., *Aquinas.* Middlesex, England: Penguin Books, Ltd., 1955.

---

[8] Quoted in *A Short History of Education,* by J. W. Adamson (Cambridge, England: At the University Press, 1919), p. 76.

Coulton, G. C., *Medieval Panorama*. 2 vols. London: The Fontana Library, 1961.

Dawson, C., *The Making of Europe*. New York: Meridian Books, Inc., 1956.

Donohue, S. J., *St. Thomas Aquinas and Education*. New York: Random House, Inc., 1968.

Evans, Joan (ed.), *The Flowering of the Middle Ages*. London: Thames and Hudson, 1966.

Haskins, C. H., *The Rise of Universities*. Ithaca, N.Y.: Cornell University Press, 1957.

Huizinga, J., *The Waning of the Middle Ages*. New York: Doubleday & Company, Doubleday Anchor Books, 1924.

Kevane, E., *Augustine the Educator: A Study in the Fundamentals of Christian Formation*. Westminster, Md.: Newman Press, 1964.

Nakosteen, M., *History of Islamic Origins of Western Education, A.D. 800–1350*. Boulder: University of Colorado Press, 1964.

Pieper, J., *Guide to Thomas Aquinas*. Translated by R. and C. Winston. New York: Pantheon Books, 1962.

Rashdall, Hastings, *Universities of Europe in the Middle Ages*. Rev. ed. Edited by F. M. Powicke and A. B. Emden. New York: Oxford University Press, 1936.

Trevor-Roper, H., *The Rise of Christian Europe*. London: Thames and Hudson, 1965.

Waddell, Helen, *Peter Abelard*. New York: Henry Holt & Co., 1933.

—— *The Wandering Scholars*. London: Constable & Co., Ltd., 1927.

West, A. F., *Alcuin and the Rise of Christian Schools*. New York: Charles Scribner's Sons, 1903.

# 4

# The
# Classical
# Revival

NOTHING IN HISTORY is simple or clear-cut. The same social changes that brought about a certain unity in medieval Christian civilization were also responsible, in time, for the great intellectual and religious transformations called the Renaissance and Reformation. These usher in the modern historical era. It is clear now that medieval unity exists more in the realm of historical theory, in the minds of some historians, than it ever did in reality. And it was in any case short-lived. But if there was one area in which unity was achieved, then it was in education. As the modern period began, Western education was under the predominant influence of organized religion. Besides its *interest* in education, the church also possessed the personnel, knowledge, and money necessary to *control* it. The effect of this control has lasted well into the twentieth century in many countries, and some would consider it to be the most important single factor underlying modern educational history.

## THE RENAISSANCE

Yet the Renaissance period does mark a new turning point in education, as in other fields. Usually the word *Renaissance* refers to the rebirth of classical studies in Europe from the fourteenth to the sixteenth century. Though medieval Christendom had already had recourse to some aspects of the intellectual culture of pagan antiquity, this interest had been extremely limited in its scope. It had confined itself largely to the work of Aristotle and the problems of its relationship to Christian doctrine. The interest we now encounter had no such self-imposed limits.

The nineteenth-century scientist T. H. Huxley remarked:

> Philosophers in the Middle Ages were allowed the high privilege of showing by logical process how and why that which the Church said was true, must be true. And if their demonstration fell short of or exceeded this limit, the Church was maternally ready to check their aberrations: if need were by the help of the secular arm.[1]

From the fourteenth century onwards, the whole of classical literary and artistic culture came under increasing scrutiny and study by Western scholars and as a result took paramount place in the curriculum. This position was maintained for hundreds of years and has been significantly varied or changed only in the past century. There are still people to be found who consider an "educated man" to be someone who has received a classical education. Before the contemporary student can assess the validity of this assumption, it is necessary to see how it came about and what it originally signified.

The Renaissance began in the towns and cities of north-

[1] T. H. Huxley, "Science and Culture" (address delivered in 1880). Quoted in *Issues in Education,* ed. B. Johnston (Boston: Houghton Mifflin Company, 1964), p. 329.

ern Italy and subsequently spread to northwestern Europe. It was the product of an urban culture, and a highly developed urban culture. The Italian cities were rather more advanced in the quality of their urbanity than even their favorable location at the growing trading centers of Europe would lead one to suppose. They had, in fact, never ceased to function as urban entities even during the Dark Ages; nor had they ceased to trade and maintain wide cultural contacts. In addition, the memory of a glorious and mainly secular past probably lingered longer and stronger in these towns than in any other part of Europe, perhaps because they were also more aware of the secular ambitions of papal Rome.

The increase in trade after the tenth century brought a great deal of wealth to people in towns who were well disposed to receive it. And by wealth is meant money. The Italian cities did not usually go in for the production of what a modern economist would regard as wealth. They were principally trading and financial cities, and the "Golden Age of the Italian Renaissance" has a literal as well as a figurative meaning. Money is a key factor in any consideration of the new culture that developed there. When, just as in the case of Spain later on, gold, silver, and inflation were imported into Europe from America in the sixteenth century, these cities rapidly declined in power and influence.

Before this happened, a new type of social leader appeared—the merchant-prince. He embodied the social and political characteristics of both the aristocrat and the businessman. At the same time as he enjoyed the taste of power, luxury, elegance, and leisure, he also displayed a capacity for enterprise and curiosity. Above all, he possessed enormous self-confidence. He patronized a great variety of activities, including art, architecture, music, scholarship, and invention. Some historians are prone to see the period in terms of its mechanical inventions, notably those of printing, the compass, and gunpowder. The first symbolizes for them the intellectual revolution, the second the penchant for travel and discovery, and the third the changed political situation. Together they underline what was new in the character of the time: the breakaway from many medieval ties in action, thought, and feeling. The accent is now on the importance of the individual, secular, and this-worldly experience, as contrasted with the collective, religious, and other-worldly emphases of the previous millennium—and this despite the fact that most people remained credulous, superstitious, and class-conscious, more frightened and disturbed by the changes than elated. The educational legacy reflects both these reactions.

### The Humanist

The humanist, as the intellectual of the period came to be called, sought after authority in much the same manner as his medieval counterpart had done. However, he could no longer find it to the same extent in the teachings and institutions of the church. He saw, instead, severe limitations in the scope of the former and obvious imperfections in the latter. As often as not, the humanist was not a churchman at all. In his quest for more meaningful values and a new cultural identity, he turned to the only other body of great secular literature of which he was aware, the classics of Greece and Rome. The Renaissance was, then, as much a result of dissatisfaction with, if not rejection of, medieval values as it was a rebirth of the values of antiquity. But, at least in the beginning, the response did not amount to a complete rejection: the humanist remained a Christian and a Catholic. One of them, Aenea Silvio (1405–65), became Pope Pius II. Such scholars succeeded in accommodating what they found in pagan culture to Catholicism and went on to establish the classical curriculum as the basis of Western education. Others used what they discovered as an intellectual springboard and were ultimately responsible for the two staple elements in the modern curriculum, the vernacular languages and the sciences. Yet, in practice, education was but little affected until the advent of the industrial revolution; the humanist ideas on the curriculum prevailed for over three centuries, though modified by the Reformation and by their middle-class adoption.

## Humanist Concept of Education

Originally, the humanist educational outlook reflected a positive and an optimistic response to the challenges of the period. Equally as it opposed the narrow, obsessive spirit of medieval scholasticism, it tried to merge the Christian virtues of faith, hope, and charity with the civilized pagan values of wisdom, fortitude, temperance, and justice. Especially was this the case in northwestern Europe; in Italy a more secular, individualistic note can be distinguished. The classics constituted a prime source of knowledge in both areas; Latin was a living language then, spoken and written by all educated people. The tremendous attention paid to grammar and literary style was a praiseworthy effort to refine and polish the main international instrument of communication, to improve on the vulgar Latin of the medieval period. Classical literature also served as a source of moral uplift, the study of which might improve the character, illuminate the social responsibilities, and refine the tastes of the ruthless, ambitious, and passionate men now arriving at the top of the social ladder. The humanists frequently wrote on the "proper education of Christian princes." It was a question, in short, of civilization, and precisely the same argument can be heard today in regard to what some people consider to be a too materialistic, even inhumane culture. In the light of its time, humanism offered a new educational goal—that of the scholar-gentleman, a well-mannered, balanced, healthy, and informed individual, able and willing to be of service to church or state whether as courtier, businessman, artist, soldier, lawyer, priest, or prince. The highly specialized and professional nature of the old education was replaced by the concept of a broad, all-around general training. Learning was now a necessary attribute for secular as well as religious life.

The kind of secular life that the humanists had in mind,

though, was for an elite group. For the most part they saw
education within the framework of a tutorial system with its
private, personal, and extremely flexible character. Even the
special court schools that emerged in Italy, such as that led
by the Italian scholar Vittorino da Feltre (1378–1446),
came much closer to the tutor-pupil relationship than anything we tend to associate with a school.

Generally the humanists favored an extremely wide
curriculum. The key aspect of all purely intellectual education was to be grammar, Latin, Greek, and even Hebrew,
because at the heart of Renaissance scholarship and teaching lay the aim of a personal mastery of classical literary
style, especially in Latin. But the classics by no means
constituted the whole of the recommended curriculum. In
addition, various humanists wanted to include logic, rhetoric, arithmetic, geometry, astronomy, history, politics,
geography, natural history, and philosophy. Religion was, of
course, still to be taught but with greater emphasis on
morality, demonstrating the necessity for courage, truthful-
ness, devotion to duty, temperance, and so forth, a morality
of an altogether more practical type than that favored by the
medieval saint or monk. So it is not surprising that most
humanist writers on education mention the importance of
physical training, including exercises, sports, and in some
cases military drill, health, and diet rules. Much attention
was given to personal etiquette. What they wanted in children was obedience, respect, quiet enthusiasm for learning,
and sincerity. The most valued mental quality was a good
memory.

On the other hand, the humanist views on the actual
teaching process were nothing if not humane, benevolent,
and kind. True, this is what might be expected from a tutor
whose charges would be the sons (and even sometimes the
daughters) of a rich, powerful, and noble man who might
later become the tutor's patron or supporter in other en-
deavors. Nonetheless, the advice of the humanists sprang
from deeper considerations than this. They were aware of
the importance of individual differences, suggesting that

natural aptitudes and interests should be fostered and encouraged. Studies ought to be made as interesting as possible, they urged, and not prolonged to the point of exhaustion or boredom. Variety should be used to maintain interest; concepts and meanings should be stressed rather than words or forms. Praise was regarded by all humanists as more effective in learning than punishment or the threat of punishment. Many attempts were made to improve the textbooks used; Erasmus (1466–1536), the greatest humanist scholar, urged the use of pictorial aids, and others suggested the conversational method of teaching Latin. Juan Vives (c. 1492–c. 1540), the Spaniard, went so far as to advocate professional training for teachers. But given the basic notion of the curriculum itself, it was probably inevitable that memorization, repetition, and writing remained the staple learning methods. How could it be otherwise, especially if it is considered that few tutors approached the caliber of Thomas More (1478–1535), whose example was the ideal one. Of greater significance was the fact that when the humanist curriculum was taken up by the middle classes, they were obliged for financial reasons to locate the teaching within the institutional framework of a school. There the personal relationship between tutor and pupil was lost, and pedantic teachers rapidly reduced the curriculum to its linguistic elements. These were taught in an authoritarian, mechanical, book- and rule-centered fashion, accompanied by somewhat brutal and boring disciplinary measures. And the central irony is that by the time the schools adopted humanist education, certain features of it had become obsolete. The aristocrats, for instance, quickly realized that the humanist educational ideal was simply too intellectual or, as we should say, "academic" for many students. Consequently, the instruction in Greek was de-emphasized, that in Hebrew virtually dropped, and only Latin completely retained. Instead, vernacular languages, estate management, dancing, and foreign travel were commonly added. The middle classes took a very long time to grasp this, and longer to emulate it, in certain limited ways.

Even the best educational ideas and practices evolve, or are created, in response to specific cultural situations. Should they be permitted to continue unchanged into different periods, these ideas can become the worst. This is what happened with humanist education, which under the auspices of overzealous and uncritical disciples was formalized and institutionalized and then degenerated into a sterile preoccupation with linguistic rules and literary forms. The name *Ciceronianism* has been given to the slavish concentration of the whole curriculum, in some instances, upon the writings of the noble Roman. In general, this tendency became stronger as the Renaissance spread, by the sixteenth century, into northwestern Europe. Here the Renaissance began in a more limited way and was restricted at first to a small group of intellectuals. In the Netherlands and in England also, the effect of scholasticism lingered longer and is more evident in the pious tone of humanist education there. "The first and most welcome part of education," declared Erasmus, "is that the youthful mind may receive the seeds of piety."[2] In his opinion, liberal studies came second, followed closely by preparation for the "duties of life" and good manners. The trading cities of northern Europe were less autocratic than those in Italy, and the new education found its way into the middle-class schools more rapidly. And to these factors must be added the effects of the Reformation and Counter Reformation.

## THE REFORMATION

The Reformation may be viewed as partly due to the emotional aridity of scholasticism and humanism. At the same time it has to be remembered that the Catholic Church had previously managed to weather the inevitable tensions between the evangelical and institutional elements present in any organized religion. Humanists such as More and

[2] Quoted [in Latin] in W. H. Woodward, *Desiderius Erasmus concerning the Aim and Method of Education* (Cambridge, England: At the University Press, 1904), p. 73.

Erasmus had found fault with many aspects of the established religion without being denounced as heretics or losing their loyalty to the church. But Martin Luther (1483–1546) embodied both the qualities of a scholar and the egoistic zeal of a fanatic believer. "If you hear me," he said to the mayors and aldermen of German cities, "you hear not me but Christ; and whosoever will not hear me, despises not me but Christ."[3] Thanks to the invention of printing, his views could be and were widely and rapidly disseminated. These factors, when added to the changed political, economic, and social conditions, combined to split the church. Among these circumstances were the increase in national feeling, the power and ambition of local princes, and the secular difficulties of the papacy. Protestantism owed much of its success as an organized movement to the fact that some Catholic monarchs were at loggerheads with each other and some of them chose to support the movement in order to preserve their secular power.

The eventual price paid by both branches of Christianity as a result of the physical struggle was an increase in the power of the state over the churches. Notwithstanding the fact that the first Protestants were as determined to have complete control over education as were the Catholics, the state increasingly became involved in education in the Protestant areas. This was because the early Protestants were dependent on the state for defense against the Catholic counterattacks. There was no immediate conflict because the secular authorities needed the ideological weapon of Protestantism in their initial struggle for independence, and it was assumed that the independent state could contain only one religion. Heresy and treason amounted to the same crime. When, however, the various differences between the Protestants themselves began to appear, the state gradually realized that loyalty could be ensured by educational control as much as by religious orthodoxy. In fact, education could be

[3] Martin Luther, "Letter to the Mayors and Aldermen of All the Cities of Germany in Behalf of Christian Schools." Quoted in *Classics in Education*, ed. W. Baskin (New York: Philosophical Library, Inc., 1966), pp. 359–60.

used to create a new secular religion of nationalism. All this took considerable time. The state originally was not anxious to saddle itself with the business of education; it was merely concerned with the loyalty of its citizens. But when such loyalty came to require mass literacy, the question of educational control was virtually over. Only the state could underwrite such a system.

### Education and the Reformation

The Protestant revolt was instrumental in another way in creating a climate of opinion favorable to universal education. This was due to the emphasis that Protestantism placed upon the individual reading of the Bible. At first this seemed to require only vernacular translations. Then it was realized that most people were entirely unable to read even those. Luther called upon municipal governments to provide schools for the common people, if only vernacular elementary schools, and even if the children could attend only for an hour or two each day. Calvin (1509–64) wanted both education and government to be taken over by church ministers. John Knox (1505–72) formulated a national school plan for Scotland.

A more indirect impulse given by Protestantism to the creation of new schools resulted from the fact that the new religion appealed especially to the urban middle class, a group who were in a material condition to build schools. It can also be maintained that Protestantism eventually aided the development of a wider curriculum in these schools. Psychologically, the religious dissent was but an extreme form of the Renaissance revolt against collective authority. Protestantism lent itself to an individual spirit of inquiry.

But the short-term effects of the new religious movement were anything but favorable to educational progress. The struggle for survival triggered a devastating European power conflict, exacerbated by fanatical ideological rivalry. Education took third place to the desire of many Europeans to exterminate each other and to the propagation of particular dogmas. More thoughtful people came to regard the schools and universities as intellectually contemptible. Many of the founders of the modern sciences—natural, social, and behavioral—did not work in universities at all. Loyalty oaths were frequently enforced and the former international character of many institutions of higher learning declined. Ideological intolerance was as detrimental to educational development in the seventeenth century as it has been during some periods in the twentieth.

As it happened, both branches of Western Christianity agreed that the classics should remain at the center of the secondary school curriculum. The Protestants perhaps took more interest in history, but there was little difference in teaching methods. Both groups eventually founded schools and universities with the idea of strengthening their doctrinal positions. For the Protestants, Melanchthon (1479–1560) established classical schools in Lutheran Germany, and Sturm (1507–89) organized the prototype of the German secondary school—the gymnasium—at Strassburg. Even Henry VIII (1491–1547) founded several English grammar schools, despite his marital and other preoccupations.

### Jesuit Education

The Catholics' response to the work of these people and others was strong. It is perhaps best exemplified by the efforts of the Society of Jesus, whose members are more commonly known as the Jesuits. Founded by an ex-soldier, Ignatius Loyola (1491–1556), in 1539, the order brought an almost military sense of discipline and organization to what became its major project—the establishment of a veritable network of secondary schools and colleges across Europe, and indeed beyond the Atlantic. What they aimed at and succeeded in was the creation of an educated Catholic elite capable of countering the assertions and criticisms of their Protestant rivals. Their zeal and devotion were equalled by their intelligence. Their famous System or Plan of Studies

(*Ratio Studiorum*) took fifteen years to prepare, but when issued in 1599 it was complete down to the minutest detail. Various versions had already been tried out in practice. The final plan lasted unchanged to 1832 and actually still serves as a basic guide for Jesuit schools in spite of certain changes. Before Loyola's death there were approximately 100 of these schools in existence; by the eighteenth century there were well over 700. There are not many similar examples in the history of education of such a successful implementation of a particular philosophy, certainly not until the twentieth century. But the Jesuits were not much interested in elementary education, and it can also be argued that the very success of Catholic school systems such as that of the Jesuits was, in a sense, responsible for holding back future educational developments in Catholic countries. The Protestant experience was not very different. The somewhat egalitarian implications, for instance, of the "priesthood of all believers" were largely ignored from an educational point of view, to await the time when the industrial revolution was to make them necessary and possible, as well as generally desirable.

## EDUCATIONAL AFTERMATH TO RENAISSANCE AND REFORMATION

Until the time of the industrial revolution, most education in Europe remained under the auspices of the various churches. The original spirit of the Renaissance largely evaporated, and doubtless many of the humanist educators would have been as shocked by the practical sequel to their ideas as they were by the extremes of scholastic pedantry. The liberating education imagined by them gave way to a specialized training in the mechanics and carefully edited literatures of dead languages, coupled with specific religious indoctrination. The role of the teacher with respect to his relationship to his student was sometimes reduced in the classroom to that of the bullying pedant lording over his fearful and bored charges, who crept unwillingly to school.

Something also happened to the sense of community and purpose originally enjoyed at the old medieval universities. They often functioned more as either social clubs for indolent aristocrats or vocational training centers for the clergy than as institutions of higher learning. Probably more damaging to learning, though, was the general rejection of the humanitarian view of people like Thomas More that society could be effectively reformed through its educational institutions, in favor of the idea that society could be controlled by them.

Yet it has to be remembered, and here there may be a parallel with our own time, that the educational changes with the greatest implications for the future that came about during this period were in the realm of informal education, via the new media of the printing press and vernacular languages. The many translations and textbooks on all subjects that gradually became available are evidence that knowledge was becoming a legitimate object of interest for anyone, not merely a specialized few. The old Greek spirit of inquiry and disputation, resurrected by the Renaissance and Reformation, did the rest. The eventual result was that an entirely new body of knowledge was to transform Western Civilization within the space of two centuries, and with it, education.

### SUGGESTED READINGS

#### Selected Primary Sources

Castiglione, B., *The Book of the Courtier.*

Erasmus, D., *The Education of a Christian Prince.*

———, *In Praise of Folly.*

More, Thomas, *Utopia.*

Vives, J. J., *On Education.* Translated by F. Watson. New York: Cambridge University Press, 1913.

(See also Selected Anthologies of Primary Sources listed at end of Introduction.)

**Other Books**

Chambers, R. W., *Thomas More*. Middlesex, England: Penguin Books, Ltd., 1963.

Dannenfeldt, K. H., *The Renaissance: Medieval or Modern?* Boston: D. C. Heath and Company, 1959.

Woodward, W. H., *Desiderius Erasmus concerning the Aim and Method of Education*. Cambridge University Press, 1904. Reprint. New York: Bureau of Publications, Teachers College, Columbia University, 1964.

————, *Studies in Education during the Age of the Renaissance*. New York: Cambridge University Press, 1924.

————, *Vittorino da Feltre and Other Humanist Educators*. Cambridge University Press, 1897. Reprint. New York: Bureau of Publications, Teachers College, Columbia University, 1963.

# 5

# Science and the Origins of Modern Education

WHAT WE CALL THE SCIENTIFIC method of thought stems from the same basic dissatisfaction with medievalism that had given rise to the Renaissance and Reformation. The classical revival only partially satisfied the growing interests and cultural manifestations of a new age. It provided a certain sense of identity and some new knowledge, but, as noted in the previous chapter, its lack of emotional appeal was a factor in the religious upsurge of the Reformation. Some thinkers soon realized that its contribution to the demand for new types of knowledge was relatively small. To these people the most admirable virtue of the ancient philosophers was primarily their willingness to think, not what they thought about nor the way in which they thought. The pedantic extremes of classicism as well as the fanatic excesses of the religious disputes contributed to what became a plague-on-both-your-houses point of view, a mood of skepticism and disillusionment with current modes of thinking that helped to create a new form of dissent, science.

## THE SCIENTIFIC METHOD

The man to whom many historians have given most credit for the articulation of the new attitude is Francis Bacon (1561–1626), an Englishman. Whether or not this judgment is absolutely accurate need not concern us very greatly. As usual there have been learned disputes about it. For us it will be enough to ascribe a name to the method of thought that Bacon certainly helped to popularize, *empiricism*. Real knowledge, Bacon asserted, begins with experience. You begin with what you know as a result of personal experience and only then proceed in stages to the unknown. You do this in a systematic fashion by collecting, experimenting, and classifying—before going on to generalizing. In the past, Bacon declared, the very opposite had been the case. The attempt to discover knowledge had begun with a priori generalizations not rooted in experience. Thus, although it had to be admitted that the ancients had been extremely good at arguing and debating, what was there to show for it, practically speaking? For Bacon, true knowledge would produce useful results, useful in terms of man and society; knowledge meant power to improve the worldly condition of man. "The end of our new logic," he explained, "is to find, not arguments, but arts; not what agrees with principles, but principles themselves: not probable reasons, but plans and designs of works—a different intention producing a different effect."[1] This was a singularly materialistic approach to knowledge in his day. He has been lauded by many historians as being the first modern man to have actually condemned the old philosophers. "In my judgment," he wrote, "all the received systems are but so many stageplays representing worlds of their own creation after an unreal and scenic fashion."[2] In fact, an empirical school of

[1] Francis Bacon, *Plan for the Advancement of Learning*. Quoted in *Classics in Education*, ed. W. Baskin (New York: Philosophical Library, Inc., 1966), p. 42.

[2] Bacon, *Novum Organum* [The New Method]. Quoted in *Classics in Education*, p. 38.

thought did exist in antiquity. Nor is it entirely without significance that Bacon's own classical education enabled him to express his ideas with great literary effectiveness. These, as a result of printing, reached a large number of people. Also, ironically, Bacon himself did little scientific work. But others did; the historical roll call of important scientists in the sixteenth and seventeenth centuries includes such illustrious names as Copernicus, Galileo, Kepler, Descartes, and Newton. By the end of the seventeenth century, science had become not merely respectable, as instanced by the founding of the Royal Society of London in 1662, but the major source of intellectual inspiration.

### SCIENCE AND EDUCATION

One of the first side-effects was an increase in the feeling that education ought to be more useful. A sense of balance is needed here, however, because even in the nineteenth century many teachers could be found to support the principle that the more useless a subject, the greater its educational value. The criterion of usefulness was implicit in the original efforts of the humanists but had become disregarded to some extent amid the religious controversies and at the hands of unimaginative schoolmasters. By the late sixteenth century, a few individuals in different countries were attempting to redefine the usefulness of a classical education, and, even more importantly, a handful of innovators were putting into practice some educational implications derived from this aspect of the scientific mode of thinking. Among the former, Milton (1608–74) and Montaigne (1533–92) advised those aristocrats who would listen that education ought to fit their sons for leadership in the world as it was and, furthermore, should be related to the actual capacities and interests of their sons. Too much emphasis on literary scholarship and classical linguistic skills, they argued, was both inappropriate and a waste of time. Should a gentleman require the services of a scholar, he could hire one. Apart from a basic language facility, in which Latin was still naturally included, the necessary subjects were practical ones such as mathematics, politics, a foreign vernacular language, geography, possibly estate management, and certainly a good deal more social polish. Much of this could be acquired through activities such as fencing, riding, dancing, and foreign travel. The story of the Grand Tour that gradually came into fashion is a fascinating and highly entertaining one, often recorded by the travellers themselves. Many a contemporary North American student makes much the same trip, even if on only "five dollars a day," for much the same educational reasons. The idea dawned on some aristocrats that education could be a pleasant, positively enjoyable experience.

At about the same time a few professional teachers, grappling intelligently with the problem of education in a school setting, began to consider what they were doing in a more empirical light. Prominent among these were Richard Mulcaster (1531–1611) in England and Wolfgang Ratke (1571–1635) in Germany. Mulcaster went so far as to envisage the creation of special colleges devoted to the professional training of teachers. He was one of the first teachers to observe that the child himself is as important a matter for study as any school subject, perhaps the most significant influence of the scientific school of thought on the practice of education. Both Mulcaster and Ratke urged the use and study of the child's mother tongue in schools, particularly in the early grades. They strongly deprecated forced learning. Their work and ideas are a salutary reminder that the practicing teacher can make real contributions to educational theory. Amid the plethora of today's "experts" this is, one suspects, too often ignored or relegated to the status of a cliché.

### Comenius

The man who, from our vantage point, possessed the most apocalyptic insight into the social possibilities open to education as a result of the new method of thought was

Johann Comenius (1592–1670). In one sense this came naturally to him, since he was a bishop of the Protestant Moravian sect. But unlike other bishops in the seventeenth century, he managed to synthesize the scientific approach to education with his own mystical vision of man and society. He overcame the Christian view of man as a wicked, sinful creature by granting him the earthly opportunity of achieving goodness, if he were properly educated. Furthermore he extended this possibility to all men and women. "God himself," he wrote, "has frequently asserted that with Him there is no respect of persons, so that, if, while we admit some to the culture of the intellect, we exclude others, we commit an injury not only against those who share the same nature as ourselves, but against God himself."[3] If the well-nigh universal ignorance of his time could be overcome, then social and international harmony would follow. Here, in effect, is the first truly democratic utopian picture of the potential benefits of mass education. Comenius in the seventeenth century envisaged a world-wide, Christian, democratic republic, bound together by a vast network of schools and universities dedicated to the pursuit of knowledge and truth.

This comprehensive education system was to be aimed at each of the three levels on which any individual operated—the vocational, the social, and the cultural. Comenius outlined a master plan whereby this could be achieved, beginning with a more positive training of the child by the mother herself. After that would come a compulsory vernacular elementary school for all children, to be followed by a Latin secondary school for those capable. Finally, the ablest would proceed to a university, though it appears that not many girls would have arrived there. Even Comenius's imagination had its seventeenth-century limits. His proposed elementary curriculum though, for girls and boys, was extraordinarily varied, and his secondary school students would have found the arts and the natural and social sci-

---

[3] J. A. Comenius, *The Great Didactic*, trans. M. W. Keatings (London: Adam and Charles Black, 1896), p. 218.

ences on the timetable. In addition, Comenius held advanced views on teaching methods and is often remembered as one of the first writers of illustrated language textbooks— the one aspect of his work that was widely taken up in his day.

Nonetheless, we return to his vision of social improvement via universal education as one of the most dynamic of the vistas opened by the scientific revolution. Considered against the turmoil, bitterness, and anguish of the seventeenth century, this was an astounding imaginative breakthrough. It foreshadowed by more than a century the concept of progress through education that largely inspires many of our own efforts in this field. Plato's ideal society, ordered by education but without the scientific vision, pales in comparison. Comenius's achievement was the merger of the elitist ideals of Christian humanism with the concept of scientific progress in order to postulate a better material and moral life for every man.

### Locke

Another instance of the early effect of the growth of science upon educational thought can be seen in the suggestions of John Locke (1632–1704), the English political philosopher. Although he directed his ideas in conventional fashion to a consideration of the most appropriate form of education for a gentleman's son, the approach is much more pragmatic. What, he asked, were the desirable gentlemanly qualities and how could an educational program promote these? His conclusion was that what counted for a gentleman were good health, virtue, wisdom, breeding, and learning, in that order. From this he proceeded to develop a fairly comprehensive rationale for most of the piecemeal suggestions that we have already noted as being "in the air." He also fired a striking verbal broadside at the traditional approach as enshrined in the grammar schools. The sole reason he could find for their existence was that the parents must "still live in fear of the schoolmaster's rod, which they look upon as the only instrument of education; as if a language or two were its whole business."[4] This led him to a common-sense examination of the psychological aspects of education, conducted within an elitist framework it is true, but which expressed a definite sensitivity to the characteristics and needs of the child. In essence Locke's advice was "be fair, firm, and kind"—unsentimental, though some would say the more valuable for that. There was no point, Locke added, in trying to force knowledge into a child. Good relations between the teacher and pupil were fundamental to the learning process. Yet Locke could not see this happening in the school situation and, like Montaigne, considered the tutorial method the only possible one for the education of a gentleman's son. A successful selection of the tutor was the crucial factor, which rendered unnecessary much consideration of what we regard as important methodological problems. There remained the question of the curriculum; but here Locke was content to restate much of what people like Montaigne had already emphasized. Thus far, in fact, Locke's importance in the history of education, apart from his fame as a political thinker, lies less in his originality than in his synthesizing abilities.

It is in his more personal analysis of the learning process itself that Locke's contribution to the new look in education mainly lies. He completely rejected the old doctrine of innate ideas on the grounds that there was no general agreement about them, which is what you might expect if they were innate, nor could they be found in either children or savages. To replace this, Locke proposed his celebrated and, as we now know, extremely misleading concept of the mind as a tabula rasa, a clean slate, on which impressions were recorded by sensual experience in the first place, and within which reflection subsequently occurred. Locke was working with the mechanical notion of science. He saw the mind as a static and passive entity, and in effect he had to

[4] John Locke, "Some Thoughts concerning Education." In *John Locke on Education*, ed. P. Gay (New York: Bureau of Publications, Teachers College, Columbia University, 1964), p. 108.

substitute for innate ideas the concept of innate powers of the mind, which comes to very much the same sort of thing as far as most people are concerned. Otherwise, it is not easy to see how Locke could have accounted for the "mind" working at all, since in his time it was still a pre-Darwinian and pre-Freudian world. He really believed that if two good-natured, educated gentlemen sat down together long enough, there were few, if any, topics on which they could not arrive at mutual understanding and agreement. Moreover, such sweet reasonableness was to a large extent a product of training and should begin in childhood with the early formation of good habits.

The shortcomings in all this need not detain us. Its validity depends entirely on the concept of a strictly limited number of educated, free, equal citizens, with strong common interests. In such a society the relationship between education and democracy is a good deal clearer than in our own. The important point is that the new method of thinking is producing a new view of human nature with enormous educational implications. Locke himself was careful to take a circumspect view of these implications, restricting his outlook to the gentleman class. But between them, Locke and Comenius had laid much of the preliminary intellectual groundwork for the educational situation that we have inherited. Locke had intimated that man was basically a good-natured, rational, and therefore eminently educable entity, while Comenius had had a glimpse of human society rendered infinitely more secure, just, prosperous, and happy as a result of an organized education system available to everyone. In some ways it is remarkable that, despite all that has happened since the seventeenth century, the optimism and faith in education generated as a result of the impact of the scientific revolution have continued in very nearly the same degree. The remainder of our survey will largely be an account of the way in which the new secular faith developed. Yet the reader would do well to bear in mind that the impact of science upon education, as in other areas of life, has been something akin, in fact, to that of Pandora's box. Once opened, it appears to have created almost as many problems as it has solved.

### The Enlightenment

The foregoing would not have been the opinion of most of the enlightened men of the eighteenth century. The view of science that rapidly gained countenance among educated men in those days was a mechanistic one. Somehow the world had been set in motion, and consequently all natural phenomena moved in accordance with fixed but discoverable laws. This is what Locke had in mind when he investigated the way in which people learn. In the eighteenth century other men proceeded along the same lines in an attempt to uncover the natural laws governing such questions as economics and politics. The fundamental law that they found most applicable to society was laissez faire, freedom, noninterference, individual liberty—it hardly matters what you call it. Of course, the people who argued in this way, although they believed themselves to be entirely objective, scientific, and rational, were actually far from being disinterested observers of the social scene. That scene in Europe was largely dominated by absolute monarchies, entrenched aristocracies, and a privileged church. The way of life of a tiny minority had attained a degree of refinement, artificiality, and luxury hitherto unknown in European experience. In order to sustain this culture, the minority interfered in every aspect of the life of the majority. The group who most resented this were none other than our old friends the middle class, and it was these people who were quick to respond to a way of thinking that appeared to provide an ironclad rationale for their grievances. They needed a theory of freedom, in short, and science seemed to supply it. So far as they were concerned, for instance, the best government was the least government, one that would leave the individual alone to decide his own affairs. Significantly, only one man dared to extend this notion fully to the field of education, and it is for this reason that Jean Jacques Rousseau is often regarded as the father of modern educational thought.

### Rousseau

Compared personally to the other eighteenth-century intellectuals, Rousseau (1712–78) appears as an outsider, a different type of man entirely, the one who "came in from the cold." Historians have described him as a rootless, neurotic, and passionate person, the product of a broken home, an unsettled existence, and a life lived continually at odds with society, whether it was that of puritanical Geneva or the incredibly sophisticated Paris salons. It is erroneous, nevertheless, to suppose that this necessarily invalidates his insight into the moral and other defects of the society he knew. In fact, the contrary point of view can be sustained, namely that precisely because he was the romantic, nonconforming rebel, he was better placed for a clearer view of society than those thinkers who had to some extent adjusted to it.

The latter tended to criticize education within a definable historical and social context. They differed from the humanists in their approach to the ancient classics. For the philosophers, classical learning was an intellectual tool that could be used not merely to criticize Christianity but to condemn it. They were not content to venerate the classics but sought to transcend them. Theirs was a consciously modern paganism, an intellectual, philosophical, optimistic paganism grounded in an analysis of history. In the words of Immanuel Kant (1724–1804), they "dared to know" for themselves. They wanted to see an end to church control of education. They favored a much more comprehensive range of subjects including science and modern history. (The eighteenth century was a great period for encyclopedias, dictionaries, and compilations of all kinds, including notably the great French work presided over by Diderot [1713–84].) More importantly, some began to stress the necessity for much wider educational provision, claiming that education could do everything for all men. Eliminate ignorance, they said in effect, and perfection, both individual and social, is within the reach of mankind. Through education all men could become more rational, more tolerant, and more humane, and they could enjoy life more, into the bargain. This has to be seen in its context. Superstition and fanaticism were still rampant. Most of mankind were still unlovely, unwashed, poverty-stricken, illiterate peasants. Europe was still what we would call an "underdeveloped" continent. So various plans for universal education made their appearance in Europe prior to the French Revolution. Yet all of these proposals remained within the common-sense Lockeian approach to psychology, and all of them were consciously aimed at the attainment of a more rationally ordered, more self-directed, civilized life. Although they were anathema to the aristocratic and religious conservatives, they represented a relatively moderate, compromise position. Many of the philosophers were aristocrats themselves.

Rousseau, because of his peculiar background and personality, saw the situation in a very different light. Also, his intention was to shock, and, being endowed with literary powers bordering on genius, shock he did. This led him to exaggerate and to express apparently contradictory and certainly confusing ideas. His originality does not lie so much in these ideas—he owed a considerable debt to the body of educational criticism built up over the previous two centuries—as in his point of view. Rousseau examined the above critique from the position of a person regarded as outside the ranks of decent, educable society, and yet one bursting with a sense of the injustice, immorality, and decadence of contemporary civilization.

As he started from the premise that the values of civilization were rotten, Rousseau was left with the child alone to consider. This was not entirely a scientific, neutral starting point, since he regarded the newborn infant as basically good, free, and equal. But what the infant became afterward was due entirely to his experience in the environment around him. In order to best preserve his good nature, education ought to impose as little as possible on the child's own curiosity, inclinations, and interests. The purer the child's nature, the happier he would be; and the aim of education ought to be that of promoting this individual potential for happiness. If achieved, then society also would become less artificial and corrupt, more natural and just. As an example of what he meant, Rousseau, in one of the most influential books about education ever written, *Emile*, outlined an ideal procedure.

### Emile

There is little doubt that he did not intend this book to be taken literally, for it is capable of various interpretations. In a sense it is merely one aspect of his overall personal onslaught against a society that was so hopelessly decadent, *Emile* implies, that no child could be properly educated in it. Similarly, the fact that Emile is brought up in the countryside can be seen as the author's method of stressing the importance of the total environment in education, something he may have gathered from Plato. Or, more simply, it can be said to reflect Rousseau's undoubted love of the countryside, a feeling like that of Wordsworth. All of these views are of little consequence, however, in comparison with the attention that his literary fiction brought to the concept of a child-centered form of education. (*Not*, it must be noted, spoilt-child-centered. Rousseau warned that the surest way to make a child unhappy is to accustom him to getting everything he desires.)

It is true that Rousseau guessed incorrectly about the intellectual capacities of children, just as it is clear that he over-romanticized Emile to the point of sentimentality. The book is full of contradictions and unresolved questions, as is much of Rousseau's other work. On a practical level the real problem of education in its relation to society is virtually glossed over in a series of brilliant, aphoristic half-truths. All we have is an absolute condemnation of the schools of his time by implication, which we have seen already, and more explicitly, from Locke. Furthermore, a close reading of *Emile* reveals that Rousseau's ideal teacher will exert a truly enormous influence and control over his pupil's development. But the author's moral and intellectual confusions must take second place to the impetus he gave to the study of the child as a new beginning point in education. By intuition alone he anticipated or rather precipitated the psychological school of educators, who, while leaving unresolved many important philosophical questions, have nonetheless radically altered many of our ideas about learning and teaching. Rousseau likewise dramatically refocussed attention on education in relation to the growth of the child, emphasized long ago by Plato but overlooked in the verbal battles concerning the proper subjects for the child to study. This concept was to attain even more prominence in the nineteenth century with the Darwinian biological theory. Nor can Rousseau's impact on the aesthetic and emotional aspects of education be overlooked—again something that had been ignored since the heyday of the Greeks. He was bold enough to assert that the aim of education ought to be to make people happy.

That Rousseau's educational impact has been something of a mixed blessing cannot be denied. It is possible that no one, except perhaps Plato or Aristotle, has been more discussed or analyzed in the history of educational thought. It has proved impossible to arrive at a satisfactory definition of what Rousseau meant by "nature," for example, as the word seems to have had a mystical significance for him. It is perhaps not so difficult to recognize his feeling of disgust with civilization; the idea that civilized life is unnatural and is inferior to the simple, spontaneous, pastoral life recurs quite frequently in history. Anthropologists seemingly point out in vain that primitive societies are actually riddled with customs, taboos, boredom, and privation, and are often tyrannical. Rousseau's lack of realism is legendary, particularly as he also wrote a letter of advice to some Polish nationalists concerning education in which he virtually contradicts what he said elsewhere. His *Emile* only makes sense on the level of allegory or fairy tale, and the kind of sense varies with the reader and the historical context. At the time of publication it was banned and burned by both Protestants and Catholics because it made the wrong kind of sense to them.

The book succeeded, as was intended, in arousing an immediate emotional response. People could not remain neutral or indifferent to his celebrated charge:

> Nothing is known about the nature of childhood. With our false ideas of it, the more we do the more we blunder. The wisest people are so much concerned with what grown-ups should know that they never consider what children are capable of learning. They keep looking for the man in the child, not thinking of what he is before he becomes a man.[5]

His was an age that can be described as intellectually shaky; the time was ripe for a new prophet, and to many Rousseau became such a figure. Rousseau was a moralist, a man with a sense of sin akin to that of a medieval monk, although he located it elsewhere. That Rousseau continues to play a stirring role in the intellectual history of Western Civilization is eloquent testimony not merely to his literary talent but to his intuitive genius for touching the sensitive nerve endings of a civilization shaken to its foundations by the dawning impact and implications of the scientific revolution. Education subsequently became an exciting new field of scientific investigation as well as of philosophical speculation. Rousseau gave it a push in both directions.

### The Psychological Movement

With the failure of the French Revolution in its utopian sense, the glow of Rousseau's ideas dimmed somewhat, at least in the popular mind. But as European society was

---

[5] Jean Jacques Rousseau, *The Emile of Jean-Jacques Rousseau,* ed. and trans. W. Boyd (New York: Bureau of Publications, Teachers College, Columbia University, 1962), p. 5.

increasingly transformed in the nineteenth century by the industrial revolution, his work continued to be a main source of inspiration for much of what was new in educational writing and practical research. And, as it became obvious that the economic changes by themselves would not bring about the perfect society, more and more people looked to education for part of the answer to the deeper problems of the emerging scientific and materialistic civilization. Thus it came about that Rousseau's views gained a new lease on life, even though as modified and interpreted by others.

The first response was naturally to see if and how Rousseau's ideas might be practically implemented. His immediate successors, Pestalozzi (1746–1827), Herbart (1776–1841), and Froebel (1782–1852), though they differed widely in areas of concentration as well as in philosophical outlook, had enough in common with the trend of his thinking to cause them sometimes to be regarded as a movement, the psychological movement. This was because they sought to base their views on practical experience with children. They all conducted schools, and, in their different ways, sought to establish a scientific base for their educational suggestions. All three were responsible for practical innovations in learning and teaching. Pestalozzi, concentrating on the importance of sense perception, particularly at the elementary school level, developed the object lesson. Herbart carefully analyzed the stages or steps of the secondary school lesson; Froebel, convinced of the fundamental learning significance of play, originated the kindergarten. Each suffered the usual penalty of original thinkers in the field of educational methods—that of having their ideas oversystematized by zealous disciples. But their combined influence has been a very great one indeed. Pestalozzi and Froebel, in particular, came close to providing a more unified conception of human nature and consequently a more integrated view of the learning and teaching process. As Pestalozzi put it: "I am trying to psychologize the instruction of mankind."[6] It must be emphasized, however, that psychology

[6] J. H. Pestalozzi, *The Method.* Quoted in *Classics in Education,* p. 527.

was in its infancy in the nineteenth century. Each of the above men brought to his study of the child certain humanitarian, moral, or religious preconceptions. It was not until our own time that educational techniques and theories came to be derived from "pure" scientific principles. The modern psychological approach to education stems from a consideration of man as simply a part of nature, a more complex and higher part than the rest, perhaps, but just as subject to the natural laws. Consequently, an immense amount of research has gone into the physiological bases of perception, behavior, learning, and so forth. As a result, education technically has made great progress. It can be very useful, nonetheless, to remember that the originators of all this were men who were guided by moral, religious, and social principles. To regard education merely in scientific terms would have appeared to them as a monstrous injustice and perversity.

### The Curriculum Controversy

No account of the impact of science upon education, however cursory, can be concluded without further reference to the curriculum debate, which came to a head in the second half of the nineteenth century. It is important to understand that the traditional secondary school curriculum, as well as that of many universities, remained largely unchanged at the beginning of this period. The study of classical languages predominated; there was little or no provision for science. To some extent the public attention that this debate aroused was due to the brilliant eloquence of the two principals involved, T. H. Huxley (1825–95), a famous scientist, and Matthew Arnold (1822–88), the poet and literary critic. But the main reason was the growing awareness of the new, industrial, scientifically based culture that had emerged already in England. It is no accident that both Huxley and Arnold were Englishmen, and no coincidence that both were deeply and professionally concerned with education. (Nor is it without significance that the issue which engaged these men was again joined in the second half of the twentieth century by the scientist-novelist C. P. Snow and the literary critic Dr. Leavis; however, the American writer Lionel Trilling has pointed out that the more recent debate has added very little to what was said by the eminent Victorians.[7])

For Huxley, the central feature of modern civilization— a feature that separated it more widely from the Renaissance than the Renaissance was separated from the Middle Ages— was the "vast and increasing part . . . played by natural knowledge." It followed that "the diffusion of thorough scientific education [was] an absolutely essential condition of industrial progress." He was, in effect, tired of being told "that the study of physical science is incompetent to confer culture; that it touches none of the higher problems in life"; and he particularly objected to the argument that "the continual devotion to scientific studies tends to generate a narrow and bigoted belief in the applicability of scientific methods to the search after truth of all kinds."[8] Herbert Spencer (1820–1903), the philosopher, not only agreed with Huxley but contended that science, in all its various branches, should be made the basis of the curriculum—a principle that has been applied in our time by the Soviet Union. Carried to its extreme, this line of thought holds that man can be more truly "liberated" by a training in the sciences than in the humanities. This amounts to using the classical rationale to justify the substitution of the sciences for the classical languages in the curriculum. It is a turning of the tables with a vengeance.

Huxley certainly did not intend to go that far. He considered himself to be "the last person to question the importance of genuine literary education, or to suppose that intellectual culture can be complete without it. An exclusively scientific training will bring about a mental twist as

---

[7] Lionel Trilling, *Beyond Culture: Essays on Literature and Learning* (London: Secker and Warburg, Ltd., 1955), pp. 145–77. ("The Leavis-Snow Controversy")

[8] T. H. Huxley, "Science and Culture." Quoted in *Issues in Education*, ed. B. Johnston (Boston: Houghton Mifflin Company, 1964), pp. 326–34, and in *Models of Man*, by P. Nash (New York: John Wiley & Sons, Inc., 1968), pp. 289–306.

surely as an exclusively literary training." His real concern was with those people "who hold that the man who has learned Latin and Greek, however little, is educated; while he who is versed in other branches of knowledge, however deeply, is a more or less respectable specialist, not admissible into the cultured caste."[9] Such a narrow view of culture and education was a betrayal of the true Greek spirit.

Huxley, in considering Arnold as the spokesman for a pedantically narrow literary education, misjudged his man. The latter had defended the pre-eminence of literature in the curriculum; for Arnold, the study of literature entailed a criticism of life, which was essential to culture. But he was not simply defending the study of "belles lettres"; that would be a "superficial humanism." The study of the classics meant "knowing the Greek and Romans, and their life and genius, and what they did in the world; what we get from them, and what is its value." In addition, he included the modern classics, which involved knowing what such people as Copernicus, Newton, and Darwin had done. He wanted to avoid "as much as possible any invidious comparison between the merits of humane letters, as a means of education, and the merits of the natural sciences." Both were necessary. What Arnold objected to was the attempt to make a training in natural sciences the main part of education. This ignored "the constitution of human nature." Knowledge by itself was not enough, he insisted; it had to be related to the human need for morality and beauty. The only exceptions he could find were the "born naturalists," who perhaps were content to collect natural knowledge. There were but a few of these people, and Arnold was concerned with universal education.

"Culture . . . seeks to do away with classes, to make the best that has been thought and known in the world *current everywhere,*" he declared (my italics).[10] Huxley agreed; he pleaded for the widest extension of education, not

9 See note 8 above.

10 Matthew Arnold, "Literature and Science" and "Culture and Anarchy." In *The Portable Matthew Arnold,* ed. Lionel Trilling (New York: The Viking Press, Inc., 1949), pp. 405–29 and 469–573.

for restricted utilitarian, political, or doctrinaire religious reasons, but because "the masses . . . are men and women with unlimited capacity of being, doing and suffering. . . ."[11] Both men looked to the state to provide universal education.

## SUGGESTED READINGS

### Selected Primary Sources

Arnold, M., "Culture and Anarchy."

———, *Culture and State: Matthew Arnold and Continental Education.* Edited by P. Nash. New York: Teachers College Press, Columbia University, 1966.

———, *The Portable Matthew Arnold.* Edited by Lionel Trilling. New York: The Viking Press, Inc., 1949.

———, *Matthew Arnold.* Edited by J. Gribble. New York: The Macmillan Company, 1967.

Bacon, Francis, *Plan for the Advancement of Learning.*

———, *Novum Organum.*

Comenius, J. A., *The Great Didactic.*

Froebel, F., *The Education of Man.*

Huxley, T. H., *The Essence of T. H. Huxley,* Edited by C. Bibby. London: Macmillan & Co., Ltd., 1967.

Kant, I., *Education.*

Locke, John, *John Locke on Education.* Edited by P. Gay. New York: Bureau of Publications, Teachers College, Columbia University, 1964.

Milton, John, *Milton on Education.* New Haven: Yale University Press, 1928.

Montaigne, M., *The Essays.*

———, *The Education of Children.* Edited by E. E. Rector. New York: Appleton, 1899.

Newman, J. H., *The Idea of a University.*

[11] See note 8 above.

Pestalozzi, J., *Leonard and Gertrude.*

Rousseau, J. J., *Emile.*

———, *The New Héloise.*

———, *The Emile of Jean-Jacques Rousseau.* Edited by W. Boyd. New York: Bureau of Publications, Teachers College, Columbia University, 1962.

Snow, C. P., *The Two Cultures and a Second Look.* 2d ed. Cambridge, England: At the University Press, 1964.

Spencer, H., *Education: Intellectual, Moral, and Physical.* New York: Appleton-Century-Crofts, Inc., 1927.

———, *Essays on Education, et Cetera.* London: J. M. Dent & Sons, Ltd., 1911.

———, *Herbert Spencer on Education.* Edited by A. M. Kazamias. New York: Teachers College Press, Columbia University, 1966.

(See also Selected Anthologies of Primary Sources listed at end of Introduction.)

### Other Books

Axtell, J. L., *The Educational Writings of John Locke.* Cambridge, England: At the University Press, 1968.

Bibby, C., *T. H. Huxley: Scientist, Humanist and Educator.* New York: The Horizon Press, 1959.

Boyd, W., *The Educational Theory of Jean-Jacques Rousseau.* London: Longmans Green & Co., 1911.

Bury, J. B., *The Idea of Progress.* Rev. ed. New York: Dover Publications, Inc., 1955.

Dampier, W. C., *A Shorter History of Science.* New York: Meridian Books, 1957.

Gay, P., *The Enlightenment: An Interpretation,* vol. 1, *The Rise of Modern Paganism.* New York: Alfred A. Knopf, Inc., 1966.

Golding, William, *Lord of the Flies.* Middlesex, England: Penguin Books, Ltd., 1963.

Heafford, M., *Pestalozzi: His Thought and Its Relevance Today.* London: Methuen & Co., Ltd., 1967.

Jeffreys, M. V. C., *John Locke: Prophet of Common Sense.* London: Methuen & Co., Ltd., 1967.

Sadler, J. E., *J. A. Comenius and the Concept of Universal Education.* London: George Allen and Unwin, Ltd., 1966.

Trease, G., *The Grand Tour.* London: Heinemann, Ltd., 1967.

Trilling, L., *Beyond Culture: Essays on Literature and Learning.* London: Secker and Warburg, Ltd., 1955.

# 6

# The Emergence of Modern Education Systems

FROM WHAT HAS BEEN SAID previously, it will be apparent that the *idea* of a comprehensive system of formal education involving universal literacy has a long history. Plato suggested it originally and 2000 years later the advent of Protestantism brought the issue up again. After the Diaspora the Hebrews began a system of education, but it was limited to religious instruction and was only for males.[1] In the seventeenth century Comenius produced his detailed scheme, and this was followed by a whole series of similar plans during the French Revolutionary era. American leaders, including Washington and Jefferson, insisted upon the importance of basic education for the young Republic. In 1717 a very different type of society, aristocratic Prussia, became the first modern state to attempt to implement a system of public schools; the king issued a decree making elementary

[1] E. B. Castle, *Ancient Education and Today* (Middlesex, England: Penguin Books, Ltd., 1961), pp. 176–82.

education compulsory for all children. Later on in the century, other Prussian monarchs issued further decrees. But with this single and doubtful exception, all these schemes remained in the realm of wishful thinking because, as Prussian experience indicated, there existed neither the practical necessity for nor the means of implementing them. Until the nineteenth century the great majority of people in Western Civilization, or in any other civilization for that matter, could have found little in schools that would have been of any *use* in their daily lives even if society had been able to afford schools.

## FOLK CULTURE

Yet ordinary people were by no means utterly devoid of culture or education. They lacked an intellectual or literary culture, but the briefest acquaintance with the veritable mosaic of folk customs, music, arts and crafts, and, above all, religious practices reveals the existence of a fairly rich emotional education and aesthetic culture, in some ways arguably superior to that possessed by many people today. This argument must not be carried too far. There is no point in romanticizing the narrow, monotonous, and often brutalized lives of poverty-stricken, credulous peasants. On the other hand, the mental picture of "folk culture" that it is possible to conjure up today, complete with overly earnest and apparently humorless young people, can be just as misleading. The culture of the folk had real artistic merits and psychological strengths. How else could people have survived the rigors of an appalling economic situation not merely with stoicism but also with a certain joie de vivre on occasions? In Catholic countries the educational role of the church, with its symbolic rituals, music, and oral literature, was of great significance, and to some extent it still is. Among Protestants the weekly sermons and church gatherings, and the hymn singing and Bible readings assumed a comparable position in the education of ordinary and extraordinary people alike. Nor can the effects of a close contact with nature be overlooked in traditional culture. Modern, industrial, urban man has become particularly sensitive to this, and not only on account of his pollution problems. One of the most stubborn difficulties in contemporary society and education is the provision of spiritual nourishment equivalent to that found in the traditional community. There is little doubt that, as yet, our schools have come nowhere near replacing the sorts of satisfaction previously taken for granted, nor is it certain that spectator sports, motorcars, and television-watching are doing so. We may also note here that traditional folk culture and modern "pop culture" are not at all the same thing. The former was largely created by the folk themselves and varied greatly from place to place; the latter is not so much created by the folk as imposed on them, and consequently there is little variety to it.

## THE INDUSTRIAL REVOLUTION

The historical phenomenon that both destroyed folk culture (or a large part of it) and also necessitated the creation of compulsory mass education systems was the industrial revolution. This drastically affected all human and social relationships, especially the position of the child. The latter had always been a part of the labor force but in a structured, stable community. As often as not, the whole family was involved in the same economic task, usually on the land. Psychologically, man seems better adapted to living in a compact group as found in the farm, tribe, or village. For the child, the entire way of life is open and apparent. Adult skills can be readily acquired through play and imitation. In the industrial society the family is usually separated during the working day. The very nature of work often becomes obscure. Growing up in huge urban conglomerations, children may have no sense of belonging and little awareness of what is important in adult life. They can, as someone put it, come to feel "psychologically double-parked." At the beginning of the industrial revolution they were in an even worse situation, that of labor units—"hands"—in factory or mine, as exploited as any adult.

However, these changes did not take place overnight. They were not at all like political revolutions, which we sometimes think of as having occurred during a particular year, or even on a certain day. Instead, 100 years were to elapse before the new social patterns were dignified by the term "revolution." Individuals had been aware that "the times they were a-changing," but the totality of the cultural transformation consequent on hundreds of small variations in the ways people earned their living largely escaped notice. It has not been until our own time that the perspective and knowledge for such assessments have existed, and even now historians still argue about it. Mass systems of public instruction were established, therefore, at a time of considerable ignorance in regard to educational problems. The gap between educational theory and practice in the nineteenth century was as wide as it has ever been in the history of Western Civilization. Much effort in the twentieth century has been aimed at bridging this gap, and it is for this reason that some awareness of how and why education systems originated is important.

### APPROACHES TO MASS EDUCATION

Unfortunately, generalizations become difficult at this point. Modern history has been largely made and written in terms of individual nation-states. The countries that shared the Western tradition differed widely in their reactions to the new conditions. Moreover, these conditions were not the same in each country, nor did they occur at the same time. There are sharp differences in the details of how, when, and why particular education systems emerged. But just as it is possible to argue that the two common criteria were those of need and possibility, so it is possible to distinguish three general approaches to the establishment of these systems in Western Europe.

### Education for Social Control

The first of these envisaged mass education primarily as a new method of *social control* and brought the state-versus-church issue to the fore. The state had begun to take an interest in education from the very beginning of the idea of the nation as the supreme political unit. The absolute monarchs, who were simply successful feudal revolutionaries, discovered the need for a corps of loyal, able, and educated civil servants in order to govern their enlarged domains more effectively. Having good reason not to trust those of their feudal equals who remained, they sought and found such people in the middle classes. As the education of this group was controlled by the church, the state began to keep an eye on it, so to speak. After the Reformation this interest was considerably strengthened in Protestant countries. Some monarchs favored the creation of local grammar schools by municipal authorities. In England, as was noted, the Tudors actually founded a few such schools and colleges themselves, besides nationalizing the church. But the overall need remained a strictly limited one. Many of the middle-class functionaries in time became aristocrats and looked after the education of their offspring in the traditional way. That the growth of nationalistic school systems from the Renaissance to the nineteenth century was such a slow process is also due in part to the international character of the European aristocracy. French, English, and so on they may have been, but first and foremost they were aristocrats. It had been perfectly possible for an English gentleman to travel to France, say, though the two governments were at war. Those were the days—if you were an aristocrat, of course.

The French Revolution changed all that. The revolutionary armies were patriotic armies, composed of men who had been led to believe that they had a personal interest in the fortunes of the French government. This was a significant departure from the former military units mostly made up of mercenaries whose leaders alone had a permanent stake in the outcome. The power of mass nationalism demonstrated by the new-style French armies was not lost on those members of the European governing classes who had felt threatened by revolutionaries at home as well as by the French. They welcomed an ideology that would bind their citizens in a common loyalty to the state—that is to say, to themselves, who acted for the state. An organized system of education was seen as the best way of inculcating such desirable feelings.

There was, however, no intention of upsetting the class structure, and the typical result of the instigation of national education systems in Western Europe is to be found in what is called the two-track system, which is by no means extinct even today. This is characterized by a more or less classical secondary school system leading to university entrance for the few, and a terminal elementary system, centered on the three R's and religious-social indoctrination, for the many. The former schools aimed at producing disciplined leaders, whereas the latter tried to turn out disciplined followers. Here the most revered qualities were humility and loyalty, in an almost medieval sense; but king and country were added to God and church as proper objects of respect and veneration. "Theirs not to wonder why, theirs but to do and die" well describes the basic attitude, except that the new social conditions demanded that the doing and dying be done more expeditiously.

### Education for Social Efficiency

At the beginning of the nineteenth century, the nationalistic social-control approach to education had little or nothing to say about the development of a *comprehensive* system of schooling for the common people. It concentrated rather on providing a more organized and standardized training for the children of the upper social classes in order to secure a better supply of civil servants and military officers. So long as the nation-state could function effectively in this manner, those who were its spokesmen were largely content to leave mass education in the hands of the churches. Even when the time arrived for the state out of necessity to concern itself with mass education, it did so with foreboding and reluctance. Who could tell where such education would end or foresee what would actually come of it? Besides, it meant increases in taxes. Cheapness was vital, and mass production methods on lines similar to those used in the new industries were favored. But it was precisely the development of these industries that was to generate a second approach to the question—that of *social* (that is to say, economic) *efficiency*. However, before we come to this, it will be convenient to note some examples of the previous approach both to illustrate and to modify some of the above generalizations.

What has been said probably applies most completely to the case of France. Napoleon (1769–1821) originated the modern French system of education and succeeded in stamping it with a character that is still recognizable, in spite of the many changes that have, of course, taken place since. Essentially he brought all educational institutions under the direct authority and control of the state. To this end he devised a highly authoritarian organizational structure. The foundations for this had partly been laid by the Jesuits, but after their expulsion from France in 1762 and the disturbances of the Revolution, the condition of educational and other social institutions was somewhat chaotic. Napoleon brought law and order, but of a very particular kind. The "University of France" grouped all secondary and higher schools into a hierarchy whose overall function was to serve the emperor. It was a distinctively elitist system, socially and intellectually; the lycées, as the secondary schools were called, boarded their students, charged fees, and concentrated on a classical-literary curriculum. Yet Napoleon's personal interests are clearly discernible: the curriculum included French, mathematics, and science; also, a few special schools devoted to medicine, engineering, science, and military studies were established. Significantly, in direct contrast to the revolutionary spirit, elementary schools were neglected; such as did exist were handed back to the order of Christian Brothers, who had previously managed them.

The example of Prussia, and later on Germany, reveals a similar pattern, but here there is one extremely important exception—the creation of the first recognizable modern university, Berlin, in 1809. Not altogether surprisingly, Napoleon's influence in the field of education also extended to Prussia. The actual development of public education there was closely connected both with Napoleon's crushing victory in 1806 and with his subsequent defeat in 1815. French supremacy on the battlefield triggered a national moral revival in Prussia, along revolutionary lines. This was eloquently articulated by the philosopher Fichte (1762–1814) in his *Addresses to the German People*, and he became the first head of the new university. For a short period it seemed as though educational reform of a fundamental type might be achieved. An exceptional individual, Wilhelm von Humboldt (1767–1835), was appointed Director of Public Instruction in 1808, and he proceeded to put into effect a whole series of changes at all levels. These included the dispatching of teachers to Pestalozzi's school in Switzerland. But he lasted only eighteen months in office, and the conservative reaction was greatly strengthened by the defeat of France. The proposed revamping of the entire system was severely curtailed. Yet Humboldt's place in the history of education is assured by his part in the founding of Berlin University. This was dedicated to scientific research; its professors and students were accorded a large measure of independence in their studies, and in the nineteenth century it became a model for university development everywhere.

England, as in so many other ways, was decidedly the odd man out in the nationalistic impetus toward education at this time. The English ruling classes, in insular isolation from Continental pressures, were content to do nothing. Education was left to the churches, philanthropic agencies, and private enterprise. The existence of a variety of religious sects certainly contributed to this attitude. But later the situation was complicated by the fact that some members of the aristocracy had not altogether forgotten that embodied in their notion of privilege was a corresponding one of responsibility. This manifested itself in concern for the spiritual and moral plight of the ever-increasing industrial masses, cut off from traditional society and doomed to "dark, satanic mills." Such concern was not widespread, was sometimes only an adjunct to the political struggle with the bourgeoisie, was of minor practical effect, and anyway contained a large measure of self-interest. Yet some aristocrats supported parliamentary attempts to regulate the appalling conditions of child labor, and these bills included certain provisions for education. Given the evolutionary character of English politics, the latter were not, in retrospect, insignificant stages in the emergence of a public system.

As the economic and political power of the middle classes grew, and as the demands of the increasingly centralized, industrial-bureaucratic state made themselves felt, so too did the view that public education would promote economic efficiency—especially when it was realized that economic efficiency was related to national power, and a number of events made this abundantly clear. In Britain, for instance, the Great Exhibition of 1851 was a dramatic illustration of the need for more widespread and better-organized technical education, if she were to maintain her industrial lead. Before 1830, provision for such training had been virtually nonexistent, and the sum of £1500 voted by Parliament in 1836 for a school of design was derisory. Annual grants were made from 1841 onward, but a marked reorganization of technical school provision took place after 1851, and again after the Paris Exhibition of 1867. Although there were many German vocational schools in existence by 1850, these had been developed by industry or municipalities. After the unification of Germany in 1871, the various German states created technological schools of a high standard. In France it was not until 1902 that the classical approach to university was significantly modified, and the fact that

France has always lagged behind in technical education is considered by some people to be partly responsible for the celebrated inadequacies of the French telephone system. The culminating example of the connection between industrial development and national power was the Japanese victory over Russia in the 1904–5 war.

The curriculum debate that accompanied the social-efficiency approach to education has, in the case of England, already been noted. Suffice it to add here that the classicists-versus-modernists issue was echoed in Germany and France in the second half of the century and, indeed, spread across the Atlantic, where it took on a new dimension. In addition, one other aspect of the efficiency approach must be emphasized: increased specialization meant increased standardization. As a result, written examinations made their appearance. They came to dominate the secondary school and university curricula. Some observers view the entire subsequent practice of education, particularly in the European countries, in terms of them. At any rate, it is no use blaming one's instructors because it is the modern bureaucratic, highly organized state that is responsible. It should be remembered, however, that at the time, the substitution of a meritocracy for the traditional aristocracy was hailed as a major social advance by liberals. In fact in England, after the terrible example of administrative inefficiency in the Crimean War of 1854–56, it was the liberal government of 1868–74 that made the civil service recruitment subject to competitive examination. The French and German systems have from their inception (the German two-track system was virtually complete by 1830) been examination-centered. And while criticism of examinations from points of view other than those of the suffering students have become common today, examinations appear to be flourishing in all countries.

### Education for Social Transformation

The third approach to mass education, although the earliest in terms of theoretical origin, was the last to manifest itself as a feasible one. This was the view of education as the means by which a complete *social transformation* might be achieved. Its emergence during the Enlightenment era has been noted, but in fact its concept of the purpose of education is not very different from that of the humanists; the aim is to "civilize." Only now, the new elite to be civilized includes the entire population. As Aristotle had remarked, a high civilization depends on the achievement of a certain level of material well-being; toward the end of the nineteenth century it was possible to imagine that this situation, as a practical proposition, was within everyone's reach. The details of the European evolution of this approach lie beyond our present purpose; they are closely allied to the political effort to achieve democratic institutions. They may be partly observed in the English Education Acts of 1870, 1876, and 1902, and in the French Education Laws of 1882–86 and 1905. In Germany the process was somewhat delayed, until after the First World War, but it is possible to argue that there was as much equality of educational opportunity there at the beginning of the twentieth century as in England and France. Reforms in each of these countries had to contend with religious and class vested interests, besides the political. More fundamental changes had to await the general shifts in social and cultural attitudes of our own time. It is more pertinent at this point to turn our attention to the New World, where the weight of tradition was either of less significance or more positively favorable to universal education. The man who first attempted to formulate a thorough educational philosophy from this third approach, in the context of industrial society, was an American.

## THE AMERICAN EXPERIENCE

That there were vast differences in the history of educational development on the two continents hardly needs much emphasis here. In sharp contrast to most European countries, the Protestant origins of American education, its local organizational base, its democratic traditions, and its universalist assumptions are outstanding elements. The combination of these features alone ensures that the story of education in America is a unique one. In addition the geographical, ethnic, social, and cultural environments cannot easily be compared with those of a single European nation. It may briefly be recalled that the original inspiration for the establishment of schools was derived from Protestant religious principles. The Massachusetts Law of 1647 required towns to set up schools and empowered them to levy taxes for their support. But such religious and educational interests waned in the eighteenth century. The common schools tended to be neglected by the local authorities, and those which did exist tended to be increasingly secularized. After the American Revolution, which had proclaimed the equality and freedom of all men regardless of class, race, or religion, interest in education revived. The practical lead was again taken by Massachusetts in 1827 by a school law that made the support of free common schools by the municipalities compulsory. This was followed by similar enactments in New York City in 1832 and New York State in 1867, but by 1852 Massachusetts had made school attendance itself compulsory. The United States was thus preceded only by Prussia in making educational provision for the masses.

On the other hand, the American practice at the secondary school level, especially on the eastern seaboard where John Dewey grew up, was not very dissimilar from European experience. Wealthy families sent their children to private schools or academies; the gentlemen of Boston in the seventeenth century, for instance, with the Indians and certainly the wilderness on their doorsteps, sent their sons to a classical Latin grammar school. The Harvard curriculum was exclusively that of the liberal arts for a considerable period (to 1825). The very founders of the United States were educated gentlemen, intellectuals if you wish, in the European tradition. Then "the roof fell in on the boys as they were working"; the action was on the frontier, and the story of American secondary education began to go its own way. Even so, it was not until after the 1860s, with the founding of the land-grant colleges, that the response to the demands of a commercial and industrial society became explicitly recognized in the curricula of higher educational institutions, and only after 1870 that the United States began to develop its characteristic free public high school system. The latter did not, in fact, become a mass institution until the twentieth century. Still, just as Prussia found a Wilhelm von Humboldt, so the United States discovered a Horace Mann (1796–1859) to advocate the virtues of public education in the nineteenth century, as well as a Henry Barnard (1811–1900), who became the first Commissioner for Education in 1867. Another important landmark was the opening of Johns Hopkins University at Baltimore in 1876; this university followed the German pattern of science and research.

By the end of the century, the effects of the industrial revolution had become as obvious in the American open spaces as in Europe. The frontier had been tamed; railroads, steamboats, and telegraph minimized differences in time and distance between the settlements. These tended less and less to be isolated, small, rural communities of homestead and farm, more and more the teeming, anonymous city. Also, the nature and size of the population changed rapidly as millions of immigrants poured in from countries that had little, if any, Puritan, Protestant, and English associations.

### The American Progressives

American social and political ideals, derived essentially from another era, began to manifest strains and weaknesses not dissimilar to the problems emerging in the more industrial parts of Europe. But in Europe the growth of democratic ideals had always to contend with the restrictions imposed by aristocratic cultural traditions and political vested interests. In America, democracy had been applied more freely and was believed in more strongly, if we overlook the South. Whereas European social critics were obliged to look to the future for a better organization of society and therefore to think in more general terms of revolution, Americans could look back to the early, egalitarian days as a sort of golden age.[2] Thus the American social critics who emerged after the Civil War could hardly be described as Socialists or Communists. They were pragmatic, elitist reformers to begin with, morally sure of themselves, who found the new political and industrial bosses crude and ignorant. They campaigned particularly for civil service reform on the lines of the British examination-based system. But the whole exuberant, optimistic, expansionist tone of American life at this time was against them. Later on a sharper, more ideological note was struck by people like Henry George (1839–97), Thorstein Veblen (1857–1929), and Charles Beard (1874–1948). Around the turn of the century the critic who aroused most public attention was the muckraking journalist, who concentrated on exposing particular social anomalies and injustices. These people were content, on the whole, to insist that the accumulation of enormous financial and political power by a few men threatened to nullify the old democratic ideals. The Progressives, as they came to call themselves, sought to rethink the meaning of the freedom ethic in terms of the new conditions. This led them very quickly to the question of education.

**Dewey**

The impact that the Progressives made on American educational thinking in general may be best studied perhaps in the celebrated series of reports issued over the period 1893 to 1918 by various committees of the National Education Association, a professional body founded in 1880. Here we shall limit ourselves to a few words on the person who did most to provide a theoretical framework for this change in attitude, John Dewey. However one regards his ideas, and like all original thinkers he has stimulated a great many

[2] T. B. Bottomore, *Critics of Society* (New York: Random House, Inc., 1968), p. 29.

uncritical and overly critical disciples and detractors, there is little doubt that Dewey stands in relation to modern education much as did Aristotle in regard to traditional education. The influence of his work has been felt in places far beyond the United States.

Hardy anyone could have experienced as fully as did Dewey the changes that came over American life from the nineteenth to the twentieth century. Born in 1859, at the beginning of the Civil War, he lived until the dawn of the electronic and nuclear age, until 1952. Consciousness of change is thus at the center of his educational thinking. It is not surprising to find that he was strongly influenced by Charles Darwin, the great biological theorist of change. The latter's theory of evolution was widely adopted to explain political and social transformations. The life process, it held, was one constant flux. The key to survival was adaptation to the material environment. In education this was translated by Dewey to mean that any new critique must contain a built-in feature of flexibility. Education must seek to give children experience in dealing with really meaningful problems, such as they would meet in life itself. To assume that children already had such experience was a great mistake. It was foolish to present them with ready-made blocks of subject matter, irrespective of any direct personal experience. It followed that education ought not to be thought of exclusively in terms of preparation for life; it was life. This notion had revolutionary implications for the school as well as for the curriculum. It challenged head-on the idea that some subjects were intrinsically more valuable than others; at the same time it suggested a basic change in the relationship between the learner and the teacher. If "useless" subjects previously taught for their supposed mental and moral disciplinary values were out, then the old frigid classroom atmosphere was irrelevant. Sympathetic cooperation should be the keynote.

The philosophical corollary to the evolutionary explanation of man and his mind was provided by the pragmatists. Theirs was less a philosophy in the usual sense than a method of thinking, but they did advance a theory of values. What they seemed to say was that there weren't any values, at least in the absolute sense. All things were relative: truth, for instance, was simply an answer that "worked,"[3] for there were no dogmatic answers to the great questions. This school of thought had a peculiar relevance for the American pioneers. They had generally found the absence of fixed ideas on any subject an advantage. Dewey and the Progressives were not so much concerned with the theory of pragmatism in an abstract sense, however, as with its social implications. For them, whatever "worked" had to work in a social context, had to be seen to work by others. This was the real standard by which men's acts ought to be judged. There was no final end to which these actions led; rather, man was involved in a Promethean, that is, ceaseless, reconstruction of the world in which he found himself. He was essentially a practical creature of action, with no fixed spiritual abode.

Both the theoretical and the more socially conscious kind of pragmatist placed great importance on the scientific method involving experiment and the accumulation of evidence for arriving at even tentative conclusions on any issue. Applied to education, this meant there were no absolute ways of learning or teaching, no eternally valid subjects, no fixed types of organizations or institutions. For Dewey the only significant knowledge was that which would enable man to master his environment. What education had to do was to bring the learner into close contact with social reality, whatever that reality happened to be. This attitude has not gone unchallenged, of course. It raises one of the most fundamental questions in modern education—the distinction, if any, between abstract and practical criteria, of which we have already seen something in ancient times. In effect, this always boils down to a dispute between those who would put the emphasis on a classical or (nowadays)

---

[3] Henry Steele Commager, *The American Mind* (New Haven: Yale University Press, 1950), pp. 100–101.

neoclassical liberal education and those who would emphasize vocational and perhaps political aims. There is no doubt that in the United States the emphasis in mass education at least has been put on the economic and political benefits. Some would argue that the impact of progressivism has had a good deal to do with this, but of course it was a two-way street. As an educational philosophy, progressivism cannot be separated from its cultural origins. One historian has suggested that Americans expect of education what they expect of religion: that "it be practical and pay dividends."[4]

Yet it appears that much of progressivist theory is not *necessarily* incompatible with the neoclassical approach to education, if it could be demonstrated that the latter approach best meets actual needs. The early American Progressives were more conscious of what they were against than what they were for. This resulted often in outright condemnation of all manifestations of authority in education, an attitude that received fresh support with the popularization of Freudian psychology after the First World War. By the late 1920s Dewey was obliged to warn some of his more extreme followers about the overly dogmatic interpretation of his writings. Critics have cited Dewey's use of vague terminology as a possible source of this misinterpretation. Now, it seemed, teachers and subject matter *had* an important role to play in education after all. The post-1950 call in the United States for a more rigorously structured and disciplined education did not, therefore, run entirely counter to progressivist theory. The important criterion for Dewey and for those with similar views was the particular social and cultural situation. This situation in the post-1950 United States was vastly different from what it had been in 1900.

Dewey was adamant in his view of democracy as the one political system capable of responding effectively to change. But democracy could only function properly if every individual was ready and able to participate in the

4 Ibid., p. 10.

political and social process. Serious doubts have subsequently arisen about both these assumptions, but these were by no means apparent around the turn of the century. Unless individuals were educated sufficiently to understand and be concerned with the problems in the complex new society, the argument ran, the democratic system was useless. Everyone was therefore entitled to the fullest educational opportunity, and the modern democratic state had a duty to provide it. And the fact was that the United States in 1900 had only started on the job of providing universal high school education.

### Critics of Progressivism

Dewey's educational views have attracted a formidable body of criticism. It has been said, for instance, that his concept of democracy and, indeed, of people in general was hopelessly utopian. To this he could have rejoined that people are good enough to merit nothing less than some form of democratic government, and bad enough not to be trusted with anything more. A more cogent and urgent comment is that most of us find difficulty in recognizing, quite apart from understanding, the complex nature of the problems that confront us in modern society. Yet Dewey allocated the highest priority in education to the individual learner. Educational conservatives argue too much so. For them the important question is, In what sense *can* education be democratic?

It remains evident that the quality of democratic life is ultimately dependent on the quality of individual citizens, and that educational opportunity is an indispensable preliminary to this. What Dewey, and certainly some of his disciples, may have done was to overestimate what formal education by itself, of whatever sort, can do in this respect. To what extent is it correct to argue, as Progressives do, that education is the fundamental method of progress and reform? Doubts have also been expressed as to whether some, at least, of those practical prescriptions popularly associated with progressive education are the best means of promoting "quality."

### Importance of Historical Perspective

So far, progressivism has had a somewhat uneven historical development; after Dewey's death it suffered something of a decline in the United States, but elsewhere there are signs of a revival in the third quarter of the twentieth century. To a certain extent this unevenness has been due to confusion over what progressivism really means. It is vitally necessary to see the movement in its historical context as well as to grasp it intellectually, to see it as a reaction against the nineteenth-century pattern of education in the United States, against the ruthless and violent extremes of individualism that Dewey had witnessed, and against the extraordinary rootlessness of American life. About the contribution of progressivism to the methodology of education, especially at the elementary school level, there is no doubt.

The movement was, it must be emphasized, but one aspect of the attempt to come to terms with the new society. The fundamental political point that the early Progressives made was the paradoxical one that individual freedom could be preserved or secured now only by more government intervention. This was the sole method by which the political and economic imbalance that existed in the United States at the end of the last century could be redressed. It is here that the Progressives link up with the European social critics. Some type of Socialism, in Dewey's opinion, was required for widescale realization of individual initiative and security. This is the perspective against which his educational views have to be seen. And although socialist theory and practice have subsequently encountered difficulties similar to those of Progressive educational ideas, their effect on twentieth-century life cannot be gainsaid. Many of the educational developments in Western countries during our time have taken place within this intellectual framework, although, of course, the national backgrounds and interpretations of it have varied greatly.

### SUGGESTED READINGS

#### Selected Primary Sources

Best, J. H., and Sidwell, R. T. (eds.), *The American Legacy of Learning: Readings in the History of Education*. Philadelphia: J. B. Lippincott Company, 1967.

Dewey, J., *Democracy and Education*. New York: The Macmillan Company, 1916.

Maclure, J. Stuart, *Educational Documents: England and Wales, 1816–1963*. London: Chapman and Hall, Ltd., 1965.

(See also Selected Anthologies of Primary Sources listed at end of Introduction.)

#### Other Books

Armytage, W. H. G., *Four Hundred Years of English Education*. Cambridge, England: At the University Press, 1964.

Bantock, G. H., *Culture, Industrialization and Education*. London: Routledge and Kegan Paul, Ltd.; New York: The Humanities Press, 1968.

Barnard, H. C., *A History of English Education: From 1760*. 2d ed. London: University of London Press, Ltd., 1961.

Butts, R. Freeman, and Cremin, L., *A History of Education in American Culture*. New York: Holt, Rinehart & Winston, Inc., 1953.

Cremin, Lawrence A., *The Genius of American Education*. New York: Random House, Inc., Vintage Books, 1966.

———, *The Transformation of the School: Progressivism in American Education, 1876–1957*. New York: Random House, Inc., Vintage Books, 1961.

Curtis, S. J., and Boultwood, M. E. A., *An Introductory History of English Education since 1800*. 3d ed. London: University Tutorial Press, Ltd., 1964.

Good, H. G., *A History of American Education*. 2d ed. New York: The Macmillan Company, 1962.

Halls, W. D., *Society, Schools and Progress in France*. Oxford, England: The Pergamon Press, 1965.

Hofstadter, R., *Anti-intellectualism in American Life*. New York: Random House, Inc., Vintage Books, 1962.

Johnston, F. Henry, *A Brief History of Canadian Education*. Toronto: McGraw-Hill Company of Canada, Ltd., 1968.

Sturt, M., *The Education of the People: A History of Primary Education in England and Wales during the Nineteenth Century*. London: Routledge and Kegan Paul, Ltd., 1967.

Ulich, R., *The Education of Nations*. Cambridge, Mass.: Harvard University Press, 1961.

# 7

# Mass Education in the Twentieth Century

AT THIS POINT we have reached the stage where the history of education merges directly into contemporary experience. To disentangle the two becomes an increasingly difficult proposition. The local contexts acquire even greater importance, and detailed studies are probably best made via comparative education. Some examples will be listed at the end of the chapter; one of the most valuable guides to *what is happening in education* is the *World Year Book of Education* series, which before 1965 was called the *Year Book of Education*. Here we shall attempt only a brief survey.

Many books have been devoted to what, after all, amounts to a profound social revolution. Western countries have become as education-centered as the civilization of the thirteenth century was religion-centered. Mass education has become the religion of our time; its temples and shrines are everywhere, and daily worship is compulsory. More than this, modern society has become dependent on the most extensive provision of education in order to function at all.

### ATTITUDES TOWARD EDUCATION

Two distinct attitudes toward our topic have become fashionable. One is to concentrate on the extraordinary developments that have taken place in mass education since its rather meager beginnings in the nineteenth century.

It is easy to be rhetorical about these changes. Never before in history have so many people been formally educated to such an extent for so long. Never before have such a large proportion of people in any society come to expect and demand education as a fundamental human as well as social right. The twentieth-century world has come to agree with Comenius that "all men should be educated fully to full humanity; not any one individual, nor a few nor even many, but all men together and singly, young and old, rich and poor, of high and lowly birth, men and women—in a word—all whose fate it is to be born human beings."[1]

On the other hand, it can be quite tempting, and is just as easy, to arrive at less sanguine if not downright gloomy conclusions. What has gone wrong? is the theme song of this school. Have the effort and expense been worth-while, in terms of the cultural benefits that earlier idealistic thinkers expected?

Neither of these attitudes, the rhapsodic or the doom-and-gloom variety, is very satisfactory as an explanation of what has happened, though as fairly common reactions they are interesting. While it is true, for instance, that the public systems have not turned out large numbers of cultured ladies and gentlemen, we have seen that this was never the intention. These systems were devised to meet the needs and satisfy the social aspirations of industrial society at a particular stage of development. Public education in the United States has, in addition, reflected local economic and racial variations. In Europe the mass systems aimed specifically at processing people into narrowly defined social, vocational,

---

[1] J. A. Comenius, *The Pampaedia*. In *J. A. Comenius: Selections,* ed. J. Piaget (Paris: U.N.E.S.C.O., 1957), p. 97.

and sometimes religious positions; mass systems there were not intended to supplant but merely to complement the existing patterns of education for the socially privileged.

The European systems, it is convenient to note, have tended to remain intact apart from certain curriculum changes. Defenders of the traditional liberal education curriculum in the selective secondary schools received theoretical support in the nineteenth century from the new-fangled discipline of psychology. Some of the early psychologists held that the mind was composed of a number of faculties, each of which could be best exercised and strengthened by a training in languages and mathematics. This was not exactly a new idea but doubtless was useful socially. Private schools in the United States, functioning along comparable lines, have not lost their attraction for those who can afford them.

In any case, there was never any *historical* reason why mass education should have resulted simply in a wider dissemination of the middle-class liberal culture of the previous century. We have already noticed that when one pattern of education is adopted by another social or national group, it does not remain unchanged. This was the case when aristocratic humanism was enshrined in the schoolrooms of the bourgeoisie and also when Athenian education was transplanted into the schools and colleges of the Hellenic period. Therefore, even if mass education *had* been intended to emulate traditional patterns, the result could not have been predicted.

A different, more useful approach to the topic is to consider the nineteenth century as marking a turning point in modern history. The term "nineteenth century" must be construed rather loosely; the intellectual momentum generated by it took some time in the present century to work itself out, though from the 1950s on, it has become clear that Western Civilization has embarked upon a new era. Apart from world politics, and unfortunately political issues can no longer be left apart for very long, developments of a scientific and technological nature—electronics, nuclear energy, automation, etc.—are altering the cultural background of education. These cultural changes form the subject of the final chapter. The point here is that whereas mass education for most of this century has had its practical and ideological roots in the nineteenth century, we know that these new developments are almost certainly of a transitional character. Much more is to come. What this will entail lies outside the province of the historian, but his awareness of continuing change indicates that he must exercise caution when dealing with the more recent past.

## EXPANSION OF MASS SYSTEMS

The most striking fact of education in the last seventy years is the expansion of the mass systems. This was a direct response to the coincidence of three factors: technological advance, social demand, and the population explosion. In practice, this has meant that the nineteenth-century idea of only elementary schooling for the masses has been enlarged in all the industrial areas to include some form of secondary schooling. Indeed, the hitherto socially sacrosanct fields of higher education are being invaded and occupied, in some cases literally. Great efforts have been made to multiply educational institutions of all sorts, though the sheer physical pressure of numbers has created major social as well as educational problems. Governments have discovered that education devours national resources at a rate exceeded sometimes only by armaments. Whereas national leaders formerly considered the iron and steel production figures of a rival, they now turn also to the latest reports of numbers and types of students produced. Given the astounding examples of Japan in the last century and Russia in this, all countries have realized what Plato and the early Protestants knew long ago—that mass education is the most effective means of bringing about fundamental social change.

In large measure the expansion has been an ad hoc response, governed by practical as much as ideological considerations. This is not to say that there has been no ideology involved, but we can say that there has been no really new ideology. Most of the ideas underlying this process of expansion originated in another era. In our period these ideas have been implemented. So far the twentieth century has not produced any overall view of civilization, culture, or human relations that can guide and inform the practice of contemporary education. It has, by contrast, produced the material realities in which mass education has evolved. This ideological gap has existed even in the United States, where the introduction of mass education, as we noted, was accompanied by more comprehensive aims and more democratic assumptions. In Europe, with the decline in class distinctions, the need not to waste talent, the greater range of subjects, and the increase in numbers of students, the educational ideology has slowly followed the American lead, to greater or less degrees.

The predominant public interest in and concern for education has been directed to the question of provision. And provision there certainly has been. But those responsible for achieving it have had to focus their attention, in turn, on administrative and managerial matters, which have become more complex as the system has grown. Education has become big business; in doing so, it has encountered much the same type of problem that huge business organizations experience. The original structures are now extremely difficult to operate, in spite of the efforts of a multitude of experts and the creation of vast bureaucratic hierarchies. Precisely the same thing can be observed in modern government. Given the best intentions, and sometimes they have not been given or have been hypocritical, this situation has not been without effect on the character and quality of mass education.

### The Economic Factor

Another important influence on educational development throughout most of this century has been the economic one or, rather, the uneven rate of economic progress. Take the depression years, for example. The most grievous setbacks to educational progress, in terms of Western Civilization at any rate, obviously occurred in those countries which succumbed to totalitarian regimes. But the democratic countries also had to curtail various reforms. One common result has been a veritable obsession with the idea of education as the key to material success both for the individual and for society. Of all the original aims of mass education, it is the vocational one that has come down to us in its purest form and has indeed been reinforced in recent years. Yet the connection between education and economic progress is, in fact, no longer as clear as was once thought. It is now known that merely to keep children in school longer does not automatically increase the gross national product. A number of additional circumstances have to be considered. In some cases, raising the age of compulsory schooling beyond a certain point is actually detrimental to economic progress. Moreover, the speed of technological change, now involving computerized, automation systems, means that it is no longer feasible to plan education in terms of manpower requirements. But these factors have penetrated public consciousness only very gradually.

### War

Another mundane twentieth-century fact of life that has continuously affected education is war or the threat of war. After both world wars the demands for extension of free education noticeably accelerated. These demands were not motivated by material considerations alone. After the blood baths, people seem to become more aware of their common humanity and approach the question of education in a more open-minded and idealistic way; the effect of the Vietnam war upon social thought in the United States and elsewhere is a recent example. These periods tend to be short-lived, if only because the economic dislocations that have followed the wars re-emphasize the material aspects. Yet there have been, alas, enough wars in this century to enlarge the area of popular speculation about education. Ironically, widespread national support for mass education has been perfected at a time when it has become apparent that the world can ill afford the luxury and anarchy of independent sovereign states. Extreme nationalism and war-consciousness have undoubtedly blighted educational development, at least from more optimistic views of what might have been.

### Theory and Practice

Such optimism has been more apparent in the United States than in Europe. It was closely related to the greater impact made by progressivist educational theories there, though the emphasis was on social adjustment rather than social revolution. Dewey has been followed by a number of able American exponents of the progressivist approach, including William Kilpatrick (1871–1965), John L. Childs, George S. Counts, and others. But, despite the deep American roots of progressivism, it is possible to exaggerate its effects even in the United States itself. The truth is that a very great variety of educational thought and practice exists in America; for instance, there is a strong contemporary body of antipragmatic thought, exemplified perhaps by Jacques Barzun, Arthur Bestor, Robert Hutchins, and Mortimer J. Adler.

In other Western countries, while socialist ideas have made demonstrable headway, progressivist educational concepts have not, though there are signs of recent interest. Consequently, that there is a necessary connection between a particular philosophical or social outlook and a particular form of education has been disputed. Certainly it is not as direct as was once thought. Catholics and Communists are as likely nowadays to disagree about educational methods among their own ranks as they are to disagree with one another about the existence of God. American Progressives have been accused of being undemocratic as equally as European defenders of highly selective, elite-producing systems. Curiously enough, there are probably more resemblances between the United States and the Soviet Union in the matter of egalitarian school structures than between both of them and most Western European countries. By and large, Europe still preserves selective schools, especially at the secondary level, though they have come in for heavy attacks in some places, notably Britain. Certainly a high economic price is paid for the wastage of talent usually involved in selective structures that are too rigid.

### Expectation

Be this as it may, there is no doubt that on both sides of the Atlantic, parents are coming to demand not only more education for their offspring but more *of* education. There is a discernible tendency to regard education as a panacea, a social, racial, political, economic, even psychological cure-all. As such traditional informal educational institutions as family, church, and locality have declined in influence, so the function of the school has increased. The parent of the obnoxious child, when summoned to the school, is quite likely to declare, "I can't do a thing with him—that's your job! What do I pay taxes for?" The modern school has thus had to equip itself with a host of specialists—nurses, doctors, dentists, psychiatrists, guidance counselors, and many others. Gradually the concept of formal education has been expanded to mean the fullest possible development of the individual, all individuals, in every respect. Needless to add, this has placed an enormous burden on mass education, and one that seems likely to increase.

### Educational Research

A more encouraging feature of the educational scene is closely linked to such social pressure. It is the dramatic acceleration in the study of education. This has now become a respectable academic subject, and modern research has made substantial contributions to the cause of educational efficiency. There are a large number of specialized professional associations devoted to every aspect of education. A great deal is now known about the learning process itself. However, the transplantation of this knowledge into the classroom has proved to be a difficult matter. Only slowly has it come to be regarded as an integral part of a teacher's education. Even here there are difficulties, but as such recognition has occurred, so the social status of the teacher has risen. The old quip, Those who can, do; those who can't, teach, has worn very thin. Teacher education is more closely connected with the university in Europe, where it was formerly under the direction of state or church. The influence of one institution in the United States, Teachers College of Columbia University, has been remarkable. Probably the greatest achievement of educational study is the well-nigh universal literacy prevailing in all Western countries today. It would be difficult, one imagines, to exaggerate the significance of this—but it has been done. The relationship between the mere ability to read and write and the attainment of a high degree of personal "culture" is also not as simple as earlier mass education idealists believed.

The extraordinary change in the attitude of adults toward children, which is such a striking phenomenon in twentieth-century education, cannot be attributed so readily to the work of the educational scientists. Rather, this seems to be due more to the material improvement in working and living conditions. Still, the humane treatment of children, advocated down through the ages by educational philosophers of all persuasions, has found strong and possibly more authoritative support from modern psychologists. In the United States, scientific child study really began with the work of G. Stanley Hall (1846–1924) on adolescence, though the value of his methods has since been questioned. Jean Piaget in Geneva has concentrated on the preadolescent child, and the psychoanalytical school, in spite of a tendency to split into often contending factions, has contributed to the better understanding of human behavior at all age levels. There is no doubt that science has revolutionized the education of the physically and mentally handicapped.

Alfred Binet (1857–1911), after some earlier pioneering efforts, established the study of individual differences, which has since flourished as a field of investigation. The concept of educability has, as a result, been greatly enlarged.

The sociologists, in their studies of the relationship between educational standards and class, status, social mobility, minority groups, and the rest, have also played a large role. The old idea that only a tiny fraction of the population *can* be educated in any meaningful sense has been considerably modified . . . but not entirely eliminated; so long as there remain wide variations in modes of family life, so too will there be variations in any given child's ability to profit from formal education. Whether or not complete equality of educational opportunity is considered desirable, it appears highly unlikely that it could ever be attained in practice. And this is without reference to the intangible question of differences in innate intellectual ability or potentiality.

It is neither necessary nor possible to enumerate the contributions of the many specialist educational disciplines here. Mention must be made, though, of the shortcomings of an exclusively or even a predominantly scientific approach to education. This has become particularly apparent in recent years when the mainstream of research has dealt with behavioral and sociological problems. One result has been a plethora of highly specialized work of a rather fragmented character. In addition, a flood of technical jargon threatens to overwhelm the subject. The student and classroom teacher, to say nothing of the man in the street, in whose behalf all this work is presumably undertaken, must be excused occasional feelings of bewilderment and frustration. More seriously, it is sometimes overlooked that this approach does not and cannot by itself answer some of the really basic questions. While science may make it possible for young Mary to solve algebraic equations, say, at a very tender age, it cannot indicate whether or not it is desirable that she should do so. Nor can it suggest whether or not we should leave it to Mary to decide.

Practical Developments

Perhaps the most fruitful lines of inquiry in the long run will turn out to be those pursued by outstanding teachers. The interested reader will readily compose his own selection of candidates, but here is something to keep in mind: even if contemporary education is mostly studied as a science, functions like a religion, and is organized as big business, its best practitioners still seem to be artists. More, some would argue, has been learned from the examples of the latter than from the efforts of those who work with rats, chimpanzees, and questionnaires. But, of course, the wise student ought not to prejudge the issue.

Any consideration of twentieth-century educational changes, however cursory cannot entirely overlook efforts to introduce technological aids into the schools. This involves more than what has been called the push-button classroom. The use of teaching machines (after the original work of B. F. Skinner on programmed learning), radio, film, language laboratories, and television has aroused considerable interest. Electronic video recordings should become as inexpensive and familiar as ordinary records. Information banks, automated libraries, and all that notwithstanding, the frequently neglected paperback-publishing revolution has surely been of profound educational significance.

Just as important as the technological developments are the various attempts to replan and restructure subjects and entire curricula. Here the overriding intention is to break away from the fragmented approaches of the past. In short, there is no doubt that education has become more efficient, and, in view of the undoubted wastage of human talent previously, this is not to be sneezed at. At the same time, the gnawing educational question remains: Efficiency for what?

Finally, positive contributions have been made by often-maligned administrators. The establishment of new types of secondary schools is the major twentieth-century development, despite a beginning made in nineteenth-century Germany with technical schools. At first in Europe most new "secondary" schools limited themselves to a simple extension of the elementary curriculum. They are, in fact, more accurately described as higher elementary schools; but gradually they have come to explore the possibility of providing a more rounded general education. In doing so they have exposed another critical problem: What type of education is most suitable for the less able student? In general (excepting the British and the Swedes), the Europeans have so far rejected the American conception of a common, comprehensive school catering to all ranges of ability. Instead, they have opted for systems that seek to isolate the more academically minded child—as the euphemism has it—from the rest. The difference in approaches was perhaps most vividly, if not altogether accurately, summarized by an American teacher after a visit to some British schools. "Your system," he is reported to have said, "produces snobs, ours slobs!"[2] But what Americans do seem to have achieved is a "continuous upward flow" to university-level work. In the 1950s and 1960s the importance of more open and flexible organizational structures became more widely recognized in Europe. Various efforts have been made to relate selection procedures to differences in intellectual capacities; in some countries the subdiscipline of testing and ability measurement has become something of a science unto itself. However, in Western European countries other than Britain, the percentage of students in higher education coming from poor homes remains extremely low.

Many other changes have been attempted in external and internal school structures, sometimes, it has to be admitted, motivated as much by parsimony as by altruism. How can the teaching resources of a particular institution or area be deployed best, or deployed most cheaply? But, just as often, changes have come about because of a genuine effort to deal with the psychological problem that is at the

[2] Quoted in W. Rudy, *Schools in an Age of Mass Culture* (Englewood Cliffs, N.J.: Prentice-Hall, Inc., 1965), p. 304.

heart of mass education. How can such education be made more human? How, that is, can it take cognizance of the many differences between individuals? Tentative attempts to answer these questions can be seen in such concepts as the nongraded and polyvalent school, team teaching, examination reform, and so on. Even the university has begun to review its teaching methods and curriculum organization; this institution has been more fundamentally affected by the problem of increased numbers of students than any other. Success here appears essential if mass education is to be able to "humanize knowledge," as Matthew Arnold would have said.

The difficulties experienced by the contemporary university have spotlighted the profound cultural changes accompanying the educational developments just outlined. It is to some of these "new realities" that we finally turn. Before the century is out, they may radically alter the process and nature of mass education as we have come to know it. Hopefully, they may contribute eventually to the reduction or elimination of the ideology gap.

### SUGGESTED READINGS

#### Selected Primary Sources

Bestor, Arthur, *Educational Wastelands*. Urbana, Ill.: University of Illinois Press, 1953.

Childs, John L., *American Pragmatism and Education*. New York: Holt, Rinehart & Winston, Inc., 1956.

Neill, A. S., *Summerhill—A Radical Approach to Child-Rearing*. New York: Hart, 1960.

Park, J., *Selected Readings in the Philosophy of Education*. New York: The Macmillan Company, 1963.

Russell, B., *Education and the Social Order*. London: George Allen and Unwin, Ltd., Unwin Books, 1967.

(See also Selected Anthologies of Primary Sources listed at end of Introduction.)

Other Books

Archambault, R. D. (ed.), *Dewey on Education: Appraisals*. New York: Random House, Inc., 1968.

Barraclough, Geoffrey, *An Introduction to Contemporary History*. Middlesex, England: Penguin Books, Ltd., 1967.

Boulting, K., *The Meaning of the Twentieth Century: The Great Transition*. New York: Harper & Row, Publishers, Inc., 1964.

Conant, James B., *The American High School Today*. New York: McGraw-Hill Book Company, Inc., 1959.

Grant, N., *Soviet Education*. Middlesex, England: Penguin Books, Ltd., 1964.

Kerr, A., *Schools of Europe*. London: Bowes & Bowes, Ltd., 1960.

King, E. J., *Society, Schools and Progress in the U.S.A.* Oxford, England: The Pergamon Press, 1965.

———, *Education and Development in Western Europe*. Reading, Mass.: Addison-Wesley Publishing Company, 1969.

Lee, G. C., *Education and Democratic Ideals*. New York: Harcourt, Brace & World, Inc., 1965.

Morrish, I., *Disciplines of Education*. London: George Allen and Unwin, Ltd., 1967.

Perkinson, H. J., *The Imperfect Panacea: American Faith in Education, 1865–1965*. New York: Random House, Inc., 1968.

Richmond, W. K., *The Teaching Revolution*. London: Methuen & Co., Ltd., 1967.

Tibble, J. W. (ed.), *The Study of Education*. London: Routledge and Kegan Paul, Ltd.; New York: The Humanities Press, 1966.

Vaisey, J., *Education in the Modern World*. New York: McGraw-Hill Book Company, Inc., 1967.

*The World Year Book of Education*. London: Evans Brothers, Ltd.; New York: Harcourt, Brace & World, Inc., 1965–.

*The Year Book of Education*. London: Evans Brothers, Ltd., 1932–1964.

# 8

# Some
# New
# Realities

Of the new realities affecting education, four areas of change have been arbitrarily selected for discussion here.

## THE KNOWLEDGE EXPLOSION

The longest-lived of the new cultural realities is the intellectual situation produced by what is popularly known as the knowledge explosion. It originated during the Renaissance with the scientific method of thinking. Its first triumph was the creation of a new language, mathematics, through which man was able to gain an unprecedented insight into, and control over, his environment. The invention of the printing press ensured that the scientific breakthrough permeated all Western countries. It is not much of an exaggeration to say that wide distribution of knowledge via the book created a new psychological type—the private, detached man who could view the universe objectively, independent of immediate social pressures. Certainly a totally new intellectual environment was born, the cult of individual enquiry and research.

However, the immediate effects were muted, or rather delayed, by the ensuing religious and political controversies. The universities and schools were not able to escape social pressures; they continued to transmit traditional culture and did not attempt to extend knowledge or question accepted ideas. It was not until after the French Revolution, in Germany, that the university became the center of scientific research. The function of the school remained the same throughout the nineteenth century; when the masses arrived, it and the teacher were still the main storehouses of knowledge. Their business was principally to pass it on:

> Cram it in, cram it in,
> Their heads are good and hollow;
> Cram it in, cram it in,
> Still there's more to follow!

In the twentieth century the accumulation of knowledge has been so rapid that the formal institutions can no longer cope with it as such. There is simply too much to know, too much to be "crammed in." Nowadays the average ten-year-old boy is quite likely to know a good deal more in some areas than his teacher. Even the five-year-old possesses a tremendous range of knowledge and vicarious experience before he toddles into the kindergarten. One effect of this has been a call for a new emphasis in school learning, a shift from knowledge per se to "learning how to learn."

It is not only the stupendous increase in quantity of knowledge, however, that afflicts the educational process but also the complex character of this knowledge. Most of the present subjects studied at university had not been invented 100 or so years ago. In addition, the study of the old subjects has been drastically altered. An old rural doctor, for example, would have great difficulty in getting through second-year medical school today unless he had made continuous efforts to keep up.

The combination of the knowledge explosion with the increase in the numbers of students is a major cause of unrest in the university. Many universities (and perhaps some of the students, too) have become highly specialized knowledge factories with little sense of community—a congeries of departments united only by a "central heating system" or a "common grievance over parking," as some witty Americans have observed.[1] This dilemma is especially acute in the United States, where the word "multi-university" originated. The problems of some American universities were still, in 1968, science fiction to a British student.[2] Everywhere, teaching in higher education centers has tended to suffer as the "publish or be damned" atmosphere engulfs the lecturers.

More fundamentally, the knowledge revolution has undermined all previous general philosophies; the "isms" have become "wasms." It seems to have precluded the possibility, for the time being, of any new views of culture that might guide, inspire, or provide values for education. The concept of an educated man has become well-nigh impossible to define at a time when such definitions are perhaps more culturally needed than ever. The best we seem capable of is the Specially Informed Man, a curious ideal compatible with absolutist and democratic forms of society. Yet without a more satisfactory goal, what are we to aim at in education? The question is particularly applicable to that majority of children who are not really capable of becoming very specially informed. Unlike the Greeks, Romans, medieval schoolmen, humanists, and Herbert Spencer, we have no clear answer to the latter's big question: What knowledge is of most worth?

It has been noted that, in the nineteenth century, Spencer had no doubt about the answer. What was important then was science. In all its forms, science should domi-

[1] Clark Kerr, *The Uses of the University* (Cambridge, Mass.: Harvard University Press, 1964), p. 20.

[2] Michael Beloff, *The Plate Glass Universities* (London: Secker and Warburg, Ltd., 1968), p. 187.

nate the curriculum. That Spencer was also aware of the possibility of a period when there would be "a great increase of spare time" is often overlooked. At that moment, he recognized, there would be a clear case for education to take more account of "aesthetic culture and its pleasures." What he could not foresee was that such a time would materialize so soon. Less than a century after his death, affluence is beginning to affect education.

### AFFLUENCE

In simple economic terms, affluence marks the shift in emphasis from production to consumption now evident in a few countries. In human terms, the age-old struggle of mankind to provide itself with the material necessities of existence is becoming a secondary concern. This is already having an effect on the vocational orientation of mass education programs. The relentless speed of technological change means that the most effective job training will be done on the job itself. Affluence has two other results of direct significance to education: one refers to the nature of work and the other, as Spencer foresaw, to the question of leisure.

The overwhelming tendency in modern industry is toward ever-greater efficiency. This means first that each job or unit of work is made as simple as possible. The ultimate goal is to have a machine do it. Many people thus spend their working hours in ever more trivial tasks—tasks that in themselves are meaningless and can hardly be said to stimulate an intelligent fly, not to speak of a literate or cultivated human being. Already this situation has called forth a multitude of psychological studies because people who are "bored out of their minds" do not make totally dedicated workers. Incentives such as status, security, and, most of all, immediate material gratification are replacing any pride or satisfaction in work itself. (Much the same is true of general education. The possession of certificates, diplomas, degrees —"pieces of paper"—is often regarded as the ultimate *educational* goal by students and teachers alike.) Any degree of enlarged rationality with which education might equip such people is more likely to be a hindrance than an asset in their work. Now young people know all about this. One of the causes for the obvious spiritual disenchantment expressed by so many of them in formal educational institutions is their awareness of the work task awaiting them.

The other result of the drive toward efficiency is that a minority of people have to undergo a prolonged, arduous, and intensely specialized period of training that demands a great deal of intellectual energy. The danger here is not that formal education will turn out bored philistines but that it will produce industrious robots. These are the people who are called upon to know more and more about less and less. In addition, the tendency of modern industrial organization is profoundly hierarchical, that is, to separate those who make the real decisions from those who carry out the basic tasks. Should teachers accept this tendency and organize education accordingly, or should they ignore it?

Some say that the answer to the emotional problems being created by certain work situations on the personal and social levels is to be found in the greater amount of leisure time now available for everyone. The majority of men will find the satisfactions denied to them in their work by means of creative activities in their free time. If this supposition is correct, it has enormous implications for education. Much of the thinking that accompanied mass education hitherto will have to be scrapped. In some respects the educational situation would then resemble that in the traditional society, except that in this case it would apply to everyone, not just a minority. But what sort of education would be suitable? As yet we do not know because no one has had to seriously consider the matter before. The struggle for existence has dominated the culture—high and low—of all previous societies. The education of those fortunate few who were born to wealth or who managed to acquire it was influenced by their awareness of the condition of the "toiling masses." It is not necessary to be a Marxist to appreciate this. We have already noted that the education of the elite was conceived both in terms of their leisure time and in terms of their political responsibilities. This brings us to the third of our arbitrary selection of new educational realities: the political.

## THE DEMOCRATIC DILEMMA

An important impulse behind the implementation of mass education systems was the extending of democratic political rights to the masses. If Everyman and his wife are to have the vote, it was said, then they need education. The only kind of democracy that had existed in the past, with the partial exception of the United States, was a limited one. Only property-owning gentlemen played an effective political role. Modern democratic thought imagined that this responsibility could be extended to everyone for three reasons: first, people were basically rational; second, a fundamental harmony of interests existed between different individuals in society, and with education everyone could be made to understand this relationship; and third, given the first two, a consensus of opinion among these rational, educated, free and equal individuals was the best and most efficient way of arriving at necessary political decisions. By the second half of the twentieth century, all these assumptions had been disputed in theory and largely invalidated in practice.

What had appeared clear and even self-evident to confident optimistic individuals who had just successfully challenged the old order in England and the United States has come to seem like wishful thinking in the conditions prevailing in modern mass democracies. Individual and minority rights have been subjected to the higher authority and power of the organized lobby, political party, and government. In fiercely competitive societies the eighteenth-century harmony of interests theory has a distinctively hollow ring to it. Differences between rich and poor, black and white, one region and another have often seemed of far greater significance than common concerns. Above all, the assumption that everyone was rational and capable of a more or less equal intellectual development by means of education seems to have been disproved, both by Freud and by the very complexity of modern political problems. Few serious political parties or advertising agencies (during election campaigns the former usually hire the latter) even dream of appealing to rational, educated humanity. On the one hand, people are deemed to be essentially irrational, subject to powerful unconscious or subconscious drives, and on the other, to be incapable of, even if actually interested in, really understanding the great issues of our time. In any case they simply don't have access to the specialized knowledge necessary to render useful judgments. All this is based, of course, on a high degree of rationalization. Current political realities thus pose fundamental problems for any sort of education calling itself democratic. The genius of American education, as Lawrence Cremin points out in the preface to his very readable book of that name, is in its "commitment to popularization."[3] At the same time, Cremin is aware that the idea of a high, nonvulgar, popular level of culture is contrary to the entire Western cultural tradition.[4] Just as modern democratic educators have to realize that modern democracy is an entirely new, even revolutionary development, so they also have to take into consideration some of the characteristics of late twentieth-century "mass culture," as it has been called. It is to this fourth "new reality" that we finally turn.

## MASS CULTURE

In the traditional society we have noted that there were fundamentally two cultures—using the word here in the sense of particular ways of thinking, behaving, and feeling. These were the folk or peasant culture and the minority culture. Essentially the difference between them turned on the question of literacy: the folk were illiterate; the elite

[3] Lawrence A. Cremin, *The Genius of American Education* (New York: Random House, Inc., Vintage Books, 1966).

[4] Ibid., p. 74.

were not. But they were not as separate as C. P. Snow imagines the literary and the scientific cultures of today to be.[5] The elite culture was in one sense a refinement of the folk culture; both shared a common religious background. The quality of the one was related to the quality of the other. Elite culture drew its sustenance from the breadth of its connection with the life of the whole community. It was certainly not the product of a coterie of snobs, highbrows, or "culture vultures": think of Shakespeare, who was appreciated by upper and lower classes alike in his day.

Mass education and the industrial revolution have wiped out the old folk culture except in those places where it continues as a tourist attraction. The early twentieth-century idea was that all people in the new industrial societies, democratic or communist, would partake of a common "high" culture, based on literacy. The question is, Has this in fact happened? Everybody is now more or less literate, but what has been the result, and why? There is considerable dispute about the answers. All that can be done here is to indicate some of the main areas of the discussion and their relevance to education.

By and large, the school is committed to quality, that is, high culture. By and large, runs the argument, modern society is not. Before we can proceed, it is necessary to have some understanding of modern society.

The picture drawn by some critics, indeed most of them, is a bleak one. They speak of a mass society, of vast, rootless, status-hungry but well-fed lonely crowds, composed of alienated individuals desperately searching for a sense of identity, for values, and for purpose. Life in the technology-dominated mass age has become dehumanized, emotionally empty, culturally sterile. The masses, seeking to allay their anxieties and neuroses, are ruthlessly exploited by a superficial, titillating, and endless series of facile, mechani-

[5] C. P. Snow, *The Two Cultures and a Second Look*, 2d ed. (Cambridge, England: At the University Press, 1964).

cal yet powerful distractions. Apparently free, people are actually enslaved. All the characteristics of modern society —centralization, bureaucracy, division of labor, large-scale organization—have made individuals more interdependent and less independent than ever. Electronic methods of communication have transformed the whole world into a "global village," where everyone knows everyone else's business and nobody cares because the individual imagination is annihilated. And if the bored majority couldn't care less, the minority who do care, the radicals and rebels without one cause but hundreds, have been driven mad, or are stupefied or impossibly naive.

On the contrary, says the opposing point of view, ordinary people have never had it so good—in every way. There is greater personal privacy and therefore more individual freedom; there is more mobility, more choice, more everything. Greater numbers of good books are being read by a larger proportion of people; the mass media bring the possibility of audiovisual culture to the previously deprived millions; folk culture, far from declining, is more active and creative than ever. Look at the number of individual hobbies; local clubs by the thousands cater for arts and crafts and sports of every sort. People are better informed; the cry for greater participation and more involvement is a healthy result of this. From this viewpoint, the improvement in material living standards is the base on which all else rests. The price of some vulgarization, if that is really the case, was certainly worth paying. Improvement is always possible and, in fact, probable.

This second argument denounces the pessimists as cultural reactionaries and holds that the latters' analysis is no more than the expression of a snobbish and obsolete form of wishful thinking. What such reactionaries want is a return to the days when the standards, opinions, and lives of the many were decided by the whims and fancies of a so-called educated, morally superior, intellectually arrogant few. And as for the folk culture of bygone days, was it not mostly an amalgam of crudities, barbarisms, and superstition?

## CONCLUSIONS

Let us admit that both of these positions have been exaggerated here. Even so, general evaluations of contemporary Western culture have been conspicuous mainly by their absence from recent *educational* discussions. In view of the extraordinarily self-conscious and self-critical character of our era, this is surely remarkable. It may be that educational changes have themselves been too numerous and too rapid to permit such discussions. If that is so, then the time is ripe now; whatever one's individual assessment, it is clear from even this brief historical sketch that there is a very close relationship between education and culture, and it is highly desirable that this relationship be reasonably clear to those concerned with education.

We can all agree, for a start, that the social and cultural position of young people has been drastically altered. They are more healthy, more independent, and more isolated than ever before. They are also, perhaps, exploiters of and exploited by a somewhat shaky older generation whose character has been molded by very different experiences.

Contemporary education exists in an atmosphere of tension and crisis, of confusion and criticism, of total involvement and colossal apathy. It may have even contributed to this situation because in concentrating on utilitarian and materialistic objectives, it may have overlooked or neglected the paramount question of human personality or "culture." It is this matter, surely, that lies behind the recent wave of student unrest. When all the immediate grievances, the absurdities, and the extremisms are disposed of, the questions the students are posing are the eternal ones. They refer to the nature of society, the purpose of civilization, and the quality of life. In a real sense they have rejoined Socrates in the Athenian marketplace. The background is to be found in the entire twentieth-century revolt against past forms of authority, morality, and culture.

The genuine achievements of public education in this

century present something of a paradox. Of necessity the process has been made more efficient and equitable. At the same time it has become infinitely more ruthless, more specialized, and more competitive. If it functions partly as an instrument for social promotion, then it also functions as an instrument for social demotion. The resulting pressures on the system are usually grotesque. Well-meaning reforms often increase these pressures and are in any case usually piecemeal, lacking any overall cultural strategy. As the masses have poured through one of the last remaining social doors, one closed to them throughout previous history, the very nature of what had lain on the other side has changed. It is somewhat like the revolution in transportation: when everyone has a car, the experience of driving is different.

One last point from the history of education may contribute to this discussion. It relates to the limits of formal education. Experience shows, time after time, that it is not what people learn directly from formal education that is of the greatest moment. Rather, it is what they learn informally both inside and outside of institutions that constitutes the more durable educational experience. In other words, it is attitudes toward learning and life itself that are really important for the individual. These are determined by the impact of the whole culture. When the culture is passing through a state of metamorphosis, as is evidently the case with Western society today, formal education is often granted a certain degree of autonomy—which can be misleading. Modern educators in their understandable enthusiasm sometimes forget what teachers in the past did not: that formal education plays a relatively small role in the total formation of a man. When the Greeks, for instance, attempted to answer the question, What education is most suitable for the free man? they took into consideration a host of matters other than those covered in school.

The roots of our educational crisis are to be found precisely in these other matters, or new realities. And for this reason we conclude that solutions to our educational problems will depend on more comprehensive responses to the emerging cultural transformation than have so far transpired.

## SUGGESTED READINGS

Bell, D., *The End of Ideology*. New York: The Free Press, 1960.

Eliot, T. S., *Notes towards the Definition of Culture*. 2d ed. London: Faber & Faber, 1962.

Galbraith, J. K., *The Affluent Society*. Boston: Houghton Mifflin Company, 1958.

———, *The New Industrial Society*. Boston: Houghton Mifflin Company, 1967.

Goodman, P., *Growing Up Absurd*. New York: Random House, Inc., Vintage Books, 1956.

Hutchins, R. M., *The Learning Society*. New York: New American Library, Inc., A Mentor Book, 1969.

Huxley, Aldous, *Brave New World*.

Orwell, George, *1984*.

Skinner, B. S., *Walden II*. New York: The Macmillan Company, 1962.

Young, M., *The Rise of the Meritocracy*. Middlesex, England: Penguin Books, Ltd., 1961.

# Index